GORDON RAMSAY'S
Healthy Appetite

125 SUPER-FRESH RECIPES FOR A HIGH-ENERGY LIFE

GORDON RAMSAY'S

contents

Introduction

Healthy eating is a topic close to my heart. I've been passionate about leading a healthy lifestyle for many years now. It started when my father-in-law signed me up for the London marathon in 2000. Back then, I was overweight and out-of-shape, but I loved the challenge and now I'm hooked. I've run every London marathon since, even a double marathon in South Africa. My personal goal is to complete ten consecutive marathons by the time I turn 45. So far, I'm on track to achieving my target.

As for maintaining a healthy lifestyle, it goes without saying that keeping fit and eating well go hand-in-hand. Any chef will tell you that we lead the most unorthodox and unhealthy lifestyles—we pick at food all day and have no time to exercise. Only on our days off are we likely to eat properly. However, I refuse to be pigeon-holed into a stereotype. With a little extra knowledge and effort, I believe anyone can make little changes that will improve their diet and everyday lifestyle.

Now, let me clarify: this is not a diet book. Those who know me know that I don't believe in faddy diets. I do, however, believe that I can prepare and serve healthy food without jeopardizing taste and flavor, or drastically changing my style of cooking. Whether it's an elegant dinner party or a simple midweek supper, a few simple adjustments are all that's needed to make our favorite meals that bit more balanced … lower in fat and calories, yet rich in energy-giving nutrients.

Choosing the right ingredients is the core of healthy eating. It's not just a matter of selecting the leanest cuts of meat and reducing the amount of fat we consume, it helps to know which ingredients are at their peak at any given time, both in terms of flavor and nutrition. Seasonality is very important to me, both at home and in the restaurants. For our latest venture in Paris, we have pledged to ensure that the vast majority of produce we use will be sourced within 100 miles of the restaurant. If a key ingredient is not available locally, then we'll simply take the dish off the menu. That's an extraordinary commitment for any restaurant!

When it comes to putting a healthy dish together, balance and moderation are key. It's not simply a matter of putting the right types of food on a plate. How the food is cooked and seasoned, and how the whole menu comes together are just as important. And I don't advocate cutting out butter and cream completely, just using a little here and there where it will really enhance the flavor of a dish. After all, a big part of living a good life is the enjoyment of food …

Gordon Ramsay.

Healthy cooking techniques

These are my favorite ways to cook food—in order to capture and retain the flavor and nutrients, without adding excessive amounts of fat.

Steam

Steaming locks in the nutrients. The secret is not to overcook the food, and to season it well. Don't rush out to buy a fancy steamer if you haven't already got one. Just upturn a small flat-bottom heatproof bowl in a large pan or wok and put a heatproof plate on top to hold the food. Surround with boiling water and cover the pan with a lid to keep the steam in. This method is ideal for cooking fillets of fish, chicken breasts, and vegetables.

Poach

I love poaching fish and tender cuts of meat, such as chicken breasts and lamb or beef tenderloins, as the meat remains so tender and moist. And you can enhance the flavor by poaching in a flavored stock. Some nutrients may leak into the cooking liquor so, where possible, I'll use it in a soup, sauce, or stew. Apart from fish and tender meat cuts, firm fruit is suitable for poaching—in a sugar syrup or sweetened, spiced wine.

Stir-fry

Once you've done all the chopping, stir-fries are a fast and healthy way to get supper on the table. Food needs to be cut into small similar-sized pieces that will cook quickly and evenly. Vegetables and tender cuts of meat and poultry are suitable. And, if you use a nonstick or well-seasoned wok or deep sauté pan, you'll need very little oil.

Griddle

Griddling and barbecuing are fun ways to cook, and I love the slightly smoky quality they impart. It is best to marinate the food beforehand, as this reduces the amount of oil you'll need for cooking. A slightly acidic marinade serves the dual purpose of tenderizing food and enhancing the flavor. Cuts of meat and poultry that take longer to cook, like chicken legs, are better precooked (by poaching or roasting), then finished off on a hot stovetop grill pan or the barbecue.

Roast

Roasting is one of my favorite ways to cook. I always brown meat with a little olive oil at high heat, either on the stove or in a hot oven, then roast it at a lower temperature. Browning improves the flavor of the meat and cooking it slowly thereafter keeps it tender and moist. If you like, you can use a roasting rack to allow excess fat to drip off a joint of meat. Always let a roast rest before carving—it makes all the difference to the succulence of the meat.

Sauté

Pan-frying or sautéeing can be unhealthy, but it all depends on the quantity of oil used. It pays to invest in a really good nonstick skillet as this will keep the oil you'll need to a minimum. You could try using an olive oil spray, though I'm not a fan of them myself. A restrained drizzle of light olive oil is all you need. Like stir-frying, it is important to use thinly sliced, tender cuts of meat.

Braise

Braising involves browning food at high heat, then slowly cooking it with a little liquid in the pan. Generally, the pan is transferred to the oven after browning, but braising can be done on the stove if you use a tight-fitting lid. I'm very fond of pan-braising—adding just a touch of water, wine, or stock to a skillet containing browned meat, vegetables, fish, or poultry, then gently simmering until cooked.

Healthy breakfast

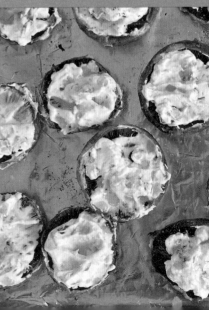

rich in vitamin C to boost your immunity

Melon and berry salad

Serves 4

1 canteloupe melon

1 honeydew melon

10oz (300g) mixed berries, such as blueberries, blackberries, and raspberries

1 lime

1 orange

1–2 tsp (5–10ml) runny honey, to drizzle

handful of mint, shredded

Halve the melons, remove and discard the seeds, then use a melon baller to carve out the flesh in balls (or simply cut it into small chunks if you prefer).

Divide the melon balls and mixed berries between individual serving bowls (or simply toss them together in a large salad bowl).

Finely grate the rinds from the lime and orange over the fruit salad. Cut the lime and orange in half and squeeze a little juice over each serving. Drizzle with a little honey, then scatter over the shredded mint.

Best served slightly chilled.

Lightly spiced
dried fruit compote

high in healthy fiber, antioxidants, and minerals

Serves 4

scant 1 cup (150g) dried prunes

scant 1 cup (150g) dried apricots

½ cup (100g) dried cherries or cranberries

½ cup (100g) dried blueberries

1 cinnamon stick

2 star anise

finely grated rind of 1 large orange

juice of 2 large oranges

generous ⅓ cup (100ml) water

2 tbsp (30ml) Grand Marnier (optional)

plain or strained plain yogurt, to serve

Put all the dried fruit in a small pan with the spices, orange rind and juice, water, and liqueur if using. Give the mixture a stir and slowly bring to a boil. Reduce the heat to low and cover the pan with a lid.

Simmer the mixture, giving it an occasional stir, for about 8 to 10 minutes until the fruit is soft and plump and the liquid has reduced and is syrupy. You may need to add a splash of water toward the end if the mixture looks too dry.

Tip into a bowl and let cool slightly. Serve in individual bowls with plain or strained plain yogurt.

Oatmeal

slow-release, sustaining energy

Serves 4

1³/₄ cups (150g) rolled oats or medium ground oatmeal

2 cups (500ml) water

2 cups (500ml) low-fat milk

pinch of fine sea salt (optional)

To serve:

4 tbsp (60ml) low-fat plain or strained plain yogurt

runny honey or brown sugar

handful of toasted slivered almonds

Put the oats, water, milk, and salt, if using, into a medium pan. Stir well, then place over high heat until the mixture begins to boil. Turn the heat down to low and stir frequently for 5 to 8 minutes as the oatmeal bubbles and thickens. Cook until it is the consistency you like, adding a splash of water if you prefer a thinner oatmeal.

Take the pan from the heat and divide the oatmeal between warm bowls. Top each portion with a spoonful of yogurt, a little honey or brown sugar, and a scattering of toasted almonds.

Also delicious eaten with fresh fruit in season, or dried fruit compote (see left).

5 ways with oats

High in fiber, oats are hailed as a wonder food for sustaining blood sugar levels, lowering cholesterol, and reducing the risk of heart disease. They are a good source of many nutrients, especially B vitamins, vitamin E, zinc, calcium, magnesium, and iron.

As they are such a brilliant source of slow-release energy, oats—in the form of oatmeal, granola, and muesli—are ideal for breakfast, because they will keep you going until lunchtime. I also like adding them to muffins, cakes, and bakes, and even savory dishes. A handful of oats mixed with fresh bread crumbs and a little Parmesan makes a fantastic crust for baked fish or chicken, for example. Versatile and easy to use, oats are an essential in any healthy pantry.

1 Bircher muesli

Put 2⅓ cups (200g) rolled oats in a bowl and pour on 1¾ cups (400ml) low-fat milk (or enough to moisten). Cover and refrigerate for at least an hour, ideally overnight.

Coarsely grate an apple over the oats, discarding the core and seeds. Stir in 1 tbsp (15ml) runny honey and ⅔ cup (150ml) low-fat plain yogurt. Add a splash of apple juice or a little more milk to loosen the mixture if it is too thick. Serve drizzled with a little more honey and topped with fresh berries and toasted walnuts. **Serves 4**

2 Granola with dried cranberries

Heat oven to 350°F (180°C). In a large bowl, mix together 2 cups (250g) jumbo rolled oats, ½ cup (50g) slivered almonds, ¼ cup (50g) pumpkin seeds, ¼ cup (50g) sunflower seeds, 1 tsp (5ml) ground ginger, and a pinch of salt. Melt 3½ tbsp (50ml) butter with 5–6 tbsp (75–90ml) honey, then add the grated rind of 1 large orange. Pour over the oat mixture and stir. Spread the mixture on a baking sheet and bake for 15 to 20 minutes until golden brown, giving it a stir every 5 minutes to ensure it colors evenly. Let cool, then stir in ½ cup (100g) dried cranberries. **Serves 4–5**

3 Banana oat muffins

Heat oven to 350°F (180°C). Line a 12-hole muffin pan with paper liners. In a large bowl, combine 1⅓ cups (100g) oats, 1½ cups (200g) all-purpose flour, 1½ tsp (7ml) baking powder, 1 tsp (5ml) baking soda, ¼ tsp (2ml) sea salt, and ½ cup (100g) light brown sugar. Mix well and make a well in the center. Mash 4 large ripe bananas in another bowl, with a fork. Stir in 1 beaten large egg and 4 tbsp (60ml) melted butter (or light olive oil). Add to the dry mixture with ½ cup (75g) chopped walnuts and fold through until just combined (don't overmix). Spoon into the paper cases and bake for 20 to 25 minutes until brown and a skewer inserted in the middle comes out clean. **Makes 12**

4 Cranachan with blackberries

Lightly toast 4 tbsp (60g) medium ground rolled oats in a dry pan, tossing frequently for 2 to 3 minutes until lightly golden. Tip onto a plate and let cool.

Whiz 7oz (200g) blackberries with about 5 tbsp (75ml) runny honey in a blender or food processor to a smooth purée. Tip into a large bowl and add 1¼ cups (300ml) fromage frais, 1¼ cups (300ml) reduced fat or regular crème fraîche, 1–2 tbsp (15–30ml) whisky, and all but 1 tbsp (15ml) of the toasted oats. Stir the mixture a few times to create a rippled effect. Spoon into glasses and top with a few blackberries and a sprinkling of toasted oatmeal for a delectable dessert. **Serves 4**

5 Oaty walnut and cheese biscuits

Heat oven to 350°F (180°C). Put 2½ cups (350g) self-rising flour into a bowl and stir in 2 tsp (10ml) baking powder, 1 tsp (5ml) fine sea salt, and a pinch of cayenne pepper. Dice 4 tbsp (60ml) butter and rub into the flour mix using your fingertips until it resembles crumbs. Stir in 1¾ cups (150g) rolled oats, 1 cup (100g) grated sharp cheddar, and ⅔ cup (100g) chopped walnuts. Make a well in the center and add 2 beaten large eggs and 9 tbsp (135ml) buttermilk. Mix until the dough comes together, adding a little more buttermilk if needed. Gently roll out on a lightly floured counter to a 1 inch (2.5cm) thickness and stamp out circles with a 2½-inch (6cm) cutter. Place, slightly apart, on a baking sheet, then brush the tops with milk and sprinkle with 1 tbsp (15ml) rolled oats. Bake for 15 to 20 minutes until golden brown. **Makes 10–12**

Buckwheat crêpes with smoked salmon

Serves 5–6

²/₃ cup (85g) buckwheat flour

²/₃ cup (85g) all-purpose flour

1½ tsp (7ml) baking powder

⅓ tsp (2ml) fine sea salt

1 tbsp (15ml) superfine sugar

generous ¾ cup (200ml) low-fat milk

1½ tsp (7ml) melted butter or light olive oil

2 large egg whites

small piece of butter, for cooking

To serve:

10–12 slices of smoked salmon

6 tbsp (90ml) sour cream

3–4 tbsp (45–60ml) capers

handful of salad leaves (optional)

olive oil, to drizzle (optional)

freshly ground black pepper

Mix the flours, baking powder, salt, and sugar together in a large mixing bowl. Make a well in the center and add the milk and melted butter or oil. Gradually draw the flour mix into the center, stirring to combine the ingredients to make a smooth batter. Let stand for a few minutes.

When ready to cook, whisk the egg whites in a clean bowl to firm peaks, then fold into the crêpe batter. Melt a small piece of butter in each of two nonstick blini pans or one large nonstick skillet, to lightly coat the bottom.

Add a small ladleful of batter to each blini pan (or two to the skillet) and cook over medium heat for 1½ to 2 minutes until golden brown on the underside. Flip the crêpes over and cook on the other side for another minute. Slide onto a warm plate and keep warm, while you cook the rest of the batter to make 10–12 crêpes in total. After the first crêpe, you probably won't need to add extra butter to the pans.

Divide the crêpes between warm serving plates and drape a couple of smoked salmon slices around. Drop a spoonful of sour cream in the middle and scatter over the capers and salad leaves, if using. Drizzle with a little olive oil and grind over some black pepper.

20

breakfast in style

the healthier option

Full English breakfast

Serves 4

olive oil, to brush and drizzle

4 portobello mushrooms, cleaned

10oz (300g) vine-ripened cherry tomatoes

sea salt and black pepper

16 slices of smoked back (Canadian) bacon

8 large eggs

dash of white wine vinegar

8 slices of rye bread, toasted

Preheat the broiler to the highest setting. Half-fill a wide, shallow pan with water and bring to a simmer. Line a large (or two small) baking sheet(s) with foil, then brush over with a little olive oil.

Trim the mushrooms, removing their stalks, then lay, cap side down, on the baking sheet. Place the vine tomatoes alongside. Drizzle over a little olive oil and sprinkle with a pinch each of salt and pepper. Lay the bacon slices in a single layer on the baking sheet (the second one if using two). Place under the broiler for 5 minutes until the mushrooms are tender and the bacon is golden brown around the edges.

To poach the eggs, break each one into a cup or ramekin. Add a dash of vinegar to the pan of simmering water. Whisk the water in a circular motion to create a whirlpool effect. Gently slide the eggs into the center of the whirlpool, one at a time, then reduce the heat to a low simmer. Poach for 1 ½ minutes if the eggs were at room temperature, or 2 minutes if they were straight from the refrigerator. The whites will have set but the yolks should still be runny in the middle.

Divide the bacon, mushrooms, tomatoes, and rye toasts between warm serving plates. Carefully lift out each poached egg with a slotted spoon, dab the bottom of the spoon with paper towels to absorb any excess water, and slide onto a rye toast. Grind some pepper over the eggs and serve at once.

Herb omelet
with cherry tomatoes

Serves 1

8–10 cherry tomatoes

1 tbsp (15ml) olive oil

sea salt and black pepper

3 large eggs

handful of mixed herbs, such as Italian parsley, chives, and chervil, chopped

Halve the cherry tomatoes or cut into quarters and place in a bowl. Heat the olive oil in a nonstick omelet pan and tip in the tomatoes. Season with salt and pepper and pan-fry over medium heat for 1 to 2 minutes until the tomatoes are just soft but still retaining their shape.

Lightly beat the eggs in a bowl in the meantime. Scatter the chopped herbs over the tomatoes, then pour in the beaten eggs. Quickly stir and shake the pan to distribute the eggs and ensure they cook evenly. When they are almost set, take the pan off the heat.

Fold the omelet, using a heatproof spatula to lift one edge and tipping the pan slightly to make it easier to fold over. Slide onto a warm plate and serve immediately.

Scrambled eggs
with anchovy and asparagus

a high protein start to the day

To prepare the asparagus, snap off the woody base of the stalks. Bring a pan of salted water to a boil and blanch the asparagus spears for 3 to 4 minutes or until tender. Meanwhile, mince 2 anchovies.

Break the eggs into a cold, heavy pan and add a piece of butter and the minced anchovies. Place the pan on the lowest heat possible and, using a heatproof spatula, stir the eggs vigorously to begin with to combine the yolks with the whites, then intermittently but frequently.

As the eggs begin to set, add a little salt, some pepper, and the chopped basil to the mixture. They will take about 4 minutes to scramble and you might need to keep moving the pan on and off the heat so that they don't get overheated. The scrambled eggs should still be soft and creamy.

Drain the asparagus as soon as it is ready and dab dry with paper towels. Divide between warm serving plates. Pile the scrambled eggs on top and drape a few anchovy fillets over each serving. If you wish, drizzle a little olive oil around the plate. Serve immediately.

Serves 4

8oz (250g) asparagus spears

sea salt and black pepper

3½oz (100g) marinated anchovy fillets (available in cartons from delis and good supermarkets)

10 large free-range eggs

piece of butter

4 large basil leaves, roughly chopped

a little olive oil, to drizzle (optional)

Stuffed mushrooms
with ricotta and walnuts on toast

equally good on a leafy salad as an appetizer

Serves 4

olive oil, to drizzle

10oz (300g) baby portobello mushrooms, cleaned

sea salt and black pepper

1½ cups (350g) ricotta

4 tbsp (60ml) chopped walnuts

1 oregano sprig, leaves only, chopped

2 tbsp (30ml) grated Parmesan

8 slices of multiseeded rye or sourdough bread

Heat the oven to 400°F (200°C). Line a large baking sheet with foil and brush over with a little olive oil. Place the mushrooms, cap side down, on the baking sheet. Sprinkle with a small pinch each of salt and pepper.

In a bowl, mix together the ricotta, walnuts, oregano, Parmesan, and a little seasoning. Spread a teaspoonful of the mixture on top of each mushroom, then drizzle over a little olive oil. Bake for 10 minutes until the mushrooms are tender.

Lightly toast the bread in the meantime. Place a couple of slices on each warm serving plate and arrange the mushrooms on top. Drizzle with a little olive oil if you like and serve warm.

Berry and yogurt smoothie

Serves 4–6

7oz (200g) raspberries

7oz (200g) blackberries

6 heaping tbsp (90ml) low-fat plain yogurt

¼ cups (300ml) milk

3–4 tbsp (45–60ml) confectioners' sugar or maple syrup, to taste

Place all the ingredients in a blender and whiz until smooth, sweetening the mixture with sugar or maple syrup to taste. Serve in chilled glasses.

more ideas for smoothies…

Fig, honey, and yogurt Trim 8 ripe figs, removing the tops, then cut into quarters. Put into a blender along with 2½ cups (600ml) low-fat milk, generous ¾ cup (200ml) low-fat plain yogurt, and 6–8 tbsp (90–120ml) honey to taste. Add 4–6 ice cubes, for extra chill if you like. Blend until smooth and thick, then pour into chilled glasses. Serves 4

Pomegranate and banana Peel 3 large ripe bananas, cut into chunks, and freeze in a plastic bag for an hour. Drop the banana chunks into a blender. Scrape the seeds from a vanilla bean with the back of a knife and add them to the blender. Pour in 1 cup (250ml) pomegranate juice, 2 cups (500ml) low-fat plain yogurt, and 1–2 tbsp (15–30ml) honey. Blend until smooth and serve in chilled glasses. Serves 4

energizing breakfast in a glass

Date, walnut, and flaxseed bread

Makes one 2-lb (900g) loaf

3½ tbsp (50ml) unsalted butter, diced, plus extra to grease

8oz (250g) medjool dates, pitted and chopped

2 tbsp (about 30ml) molasses

1 cup (250ml) water

1¾ cups (250g) all-purpose flour

1½ cups (250g) whole wheat flour

½ tsp (2ml) fine sea salt

scant ¾ cup (125g) light brown sugar

2 tsp (10ml) baking powder

2 large eggs, lightly beaten

1 tsp (5ml) vanilla extract

⅓ cup (50g) chopped walnuts

1oz (30g) flaxseed

Heat the oven to 325°F (170°C). Butter a 2-lb (900g) loaf pan, preferably nonstick. Put the butter, chopped dates, molasses, and water in a small pan over low heat. Stir until the butter and molasses have melted, then take off the heat and let cool.

Put the flours, salt, sugar, and baking powder into a large mixing bowl and stir to combine. Make a well in the center. Add the eggs and vanilla extract, then pour the date mixture into the well. Fold through the ingredients until evenly incorporated, but don't overmix. Finally, fold through the chopped walnuts and flaxseed.

Spoon the mixture into the prepared pan and spread evenly. Bake for about 1 hour until a skewer inserted into the center of the loaf comes out clean. Turn out onto a wire rack and let cool completely before slicing.

Delicious served just as it is, or lightly toasted with cheese.

Seeded honey loaf

enriched with nutrient-packed seeds

Makes two 1-lb (500g) loaves

½oz (15g) fresh yeast (or ¼oz/7g sachet active dry yeast)

scant 1¼ cups (275ml) tepid water

1⅓ cups (225g) whole wheat flour

scant 1¾ cups (225g) strong white flour, plus extra to dust

1½ tsp (7ml) fine sea salt

1¾oz (50g) mixed seeds (about 2 tsp/10ml each of poppy, sesame, pumpkin, flaxseed, and sunflower)

3 tbsp (45ml) olive oil, plus extra to oil

2 tbsp (30ml) honey

2 tbsp (30ml) milk, to glaze

If using fresh yeast, put 3–4 tbsp (45–60ml) of the water into a warm bowl, crumble in the yeast, and stir to dissolve. Let sponge for a few minutes.

Put the flours and salt into a large mixing bowl, add the seeds, and stir to mix. (If you're using active dry yeast, stir this into the flour mixture.) Make a well in the center and add the olive oil, honey, yeast mixture, and remaining water (all of it if using dried yeast). Stir with a wooden spoon to combine, adding more flour if the dough seems too wet. It should be soft, but not sticky.

Press the dough into a ball, then knead on a lightly floured counter for about 5 to 10 minutes until smooth. Place in a lightly oiled bowl, cover with lightly oiled plastic wrap, and let the dough rise in a warm part of the kitchen for an hour or so until doubled in size.

Punch the dough down on a lightly floured counter and knead it lightly. Divide into two pieces and shape each one into a round loaf. Place each on a lightly oiled large baking sheet and cover with lightly oiledplastic wrap. Let prove in a warm spot until almost doubled in size.

Heat the oven to 400°F (200°C). Remove the plastic wrap and brush a thin layer of milk over the loaves. Bake for about 20 to 25 minutes until light golden in color. The loaves should sound hollow when tapped underside. Let cool on a rack. Best served slightly warm.

Whole wheat blueberry muffins

deliciously moist and full of goodness

Makes 12

2 very ripe large bananas

scant 2 cups (300g) whole wheat flour

1½ tsp (7ml) baking powder

1 tsp (5ml) baking soda

pinch of fine sea salt

½ cup (100g) light brown sugar

scant 1¼ cups (284ml) buttermilk

1 large egg, lightly beaten

⅓ cup (75ml) light olive oil (or melted butter)

7oz (200g) blueberries, rinsed and drained

1 tbsp (15ml) raw brown sugar

Heat the oven to 350°F (180°C). Line a 12-hole muffin pan with muffin cases. Peel the bananas and mash in a bowl, using a fork.

Mix the flour, baking powder, baking soda, salt, and brown sugar together in a large mixing bowl. Make a well in the center and add the buttermilk, egg, olive oil, and bananas. Quickly fold the ingredients together until just incorporated, taking care not to overmix. Tip in the blueberries and give the batter one or two stirs.

Spoon the batter into the muffin cases and sprinkle with the raw brown sugar. The cases will be quite full. Bake in the oven for about 20 to 25 minutes until well risen and golden brown on top; a skewer inserted into the center of the muffin should emerge clean.

Let cool in the pan for a couple of minutes, then transfer to a rack to cool completely.

getting the right balance

A varied diet that includes lots of different foods helps to ensure you are getting all the nutrients you need, but the proportion of those foods on your plate is also important. It's a matter of eating the right amount from each of the food groups: carbs; fruit and veg; protein foods; dairy foods (or equivalents); sugars, and fats. It seems obvious, but not everyone has an awareness of what and how much they should be eating in a day.

Carbohydrates should provide the bulk of our food—about 50 percent of it. These give us the energy we need and the best choices are unrefined and fiber-rich carbohydrates, such as whole grain bread, cereals and rice, potatoes, and oats.

Fruit and vegetables should comprise around a third of our food intake. These are vital sources of vitamins, minerals, and fiber. The recommended amount is at least five portions a day (see pages 58–9). It's really not that difficult to achieve this.

Protein foods are vital to carnivores and vegetarians alike. We all need proteins to build and repair our bodies. These can come from fish, meat, poultry, eggs, beans, nuts, and seeds. The idea is to eat a moderate amount each day, to make up around 10–15 percent of our total intake.

Dairy products (other than butter and margarine, which are classed as fats) are an important source of calcium—vital to maintaining healthy bones—and protein. If you are lactose intolerant, goat, sheep's, and soy milk products are good alternatives. Choose reduced-fat milk and cheeses if you are controlling your calorie and fat intake.

Fats and sugars should be eaten sparingly, as we all know. Some fats are vital to health though, so it helps to understand the different types (see pages 108–9). Keep saturated and trans fats, as well as refined sugars, to a minimum.

Healthy brunch/lunch

Cod and tomato chowder

Serves 4–5

3 tbsp (45ml) olive oil

2 medium onions, peeled and roughly chopped

2 celery stalks, trimmed and roughly chopped

sea salt and black pepper

2 large carrots, peeled and roughly chopped

2 large waxy potatoes, about 14oz (400g), peeled and roughly chopped

1 sweet yellow pepper, cored, seeded, and roughly chopped

few thyme sprigs

1 bay leaf

14oz (398g) can chopped tomatoes

3½ cups (900ml) fish or chicken stock (see pages 248–9)

5oz (150g) green beans, cut into short lengths

2 zucchini, roughly chopped

few dashes of Tabasco sauce (optional)

1⅓lb (600g) cod fillets, skinned and pin-boned

bunch of Italian parsley, roughly chopped

Heat the olive oil in a heavy pan. Add the onions, celery, and some seasoning, and cook, stirring, over medium heat for 6 to 8 minutes to soften. Add the carrots, potatoes, sweet yellow pepper, and herbs, and sauté for 5 minutes until the vegetables are lightly golden.

Add the tomatoes to the pan and pour in the stock. Cover and simmer for about 7 to 9 minutes until the vegetables are tender. Now tip in the green beans and zucchini, give the mixture a stir, and simmer for another 3 minutes. Check the seasoning, adding a few dashes of Tabasco to spice up the chowder if you like.

Lightly season the cod fillets and lay them on the vegetables in the pan. Cover the pan again and simmer for 3 to 4 minutes until the fish is opaque and just cooked through.

Using a spoon, gently break the fish into large flakes. Ladle the hot soup into warm bowls and scatter a handful of chopped parsley over each serving.

satisfying and highly nutritious

Persian-style onion soup

flavanoid-rich onions help to keep the body healthy

Serves 4

3 tbsp (45ml) olive oil

5 large onions, peeled and thinly sliced

sea salt and black pepper

½ tsp (2ml) ground turmeric

½ tsp (2ml) fenugreek seeds

½ tsp (2ml) dried mint

2 tbsp (30ml) all-purpose flour

3 cups (700ml) vegetable or chicken stock (see pages 248–9)

1 cinnamon stick

juice of 1 lemon

1 tsp (5ml) superfine sugar

few Italian parsley sprigs, chopped

Place a heavy pan over medium heat. Add 2 tbsp (30ml) olive oil, the onions, and some seasoning. Cover and sweat for 12 to 15 minutes until the onions are soft, lifting the lid and stirring occasionally. Remove the lid and increase the heat very slightly.

Add the spices, dried mint, and remaining oil, then stir in the flour. Cook, stirring frequently, for 3 to 4 minutes. Gradually pour in the stock, whisking as you do so to prevent any lumps forming. When it has all been added, drop in the cinnamon stick and simmer over low heat, partially covered with the lid, for 30 to 40 minutes.

Stir in the lemon juice and sugar, then taste and adjust the seasoning. Discard the cinnamon stick. Ladle the soup into warm bowls and sprinkle over the parsley to serve.

rich in vitamin C
and healthy antioxidants

Smoked trout, orange and wild arugula salad

Serves 4

3 oranges

4 tbsp (60ml) extra-virgin olive oil, to drizzle

sea salt and black pepper

7oz (200g) wild arugula leaves, washed

2 hot smoked trout fillets, about 4oz (125g) each

To segment the oranges, cut off the top and bottom of one and stand it upright on a board. Cut along the curve of the fruit to remove the skin and white pith, exposing the flesh. Now hold the orange over a strainer set on top of a bowl and cut out the segments, letting each one drop into the strainer as you go along. Finally, squeeze the membrane over the strainer to extract as much juice as possible. Repeat with the remaining oranges, then tip the segments into another bowl.

For the dressing, add the olive oil and a little seasoning to the orange juice that you've collected in the bowl and whisk to combine.

Add the arugula to the orange segments, then flake the smoked trout into the bowl. Add the dressing and toss gently with your hands. Pile onto individual plates and serve with pumpernickel or rye bread.

Devilled Caesar salad with prosciutto

Serves 4

8 slices of prosciutto

tiny drizzle of olive oil

8 thick slices of ciabatta

4 Boston lettuce, trimmed and washed

15–16 (about 2oz/60g) marinated fresh anchovy fillets

Parmesan shavings, to finish

Dressing:

1 garlic clove, peeled and crushed

2 salted anchovies, rinsed, drained, and minced

½ tsp (2ml) paprika

few dashes of Worcestershire sauce

generous ⅓ cup (100g) plain yogurt

freshly ground black pepper

To make the dressing, whiz all the ingredients together in a food processor, seasoning with pepper to taste. You'll probably find that the anchovies provide enough salt.

Cook the prosciutto in two batches. Heat a tiny drizzle of olive oil in a nonstick skillet and lay half of the ham slices in the skillet. Pan-fry over medium heat for a couple of minutes on each side until golden brown, then transfer to a plate. Cook the rest in the same way. Leave until cool and crisp, then break the prosciutto slices into smaller pieces.

Lightly toast the ciabatta slices in the same skillet, turning to color both sides. Remove and cut into chunky croutons. Separate the lettuce leaves and divide between serving plates. Sprinkle over the croutons, prosciutto, and anchovies. Drizzle over the dressing and sprinkle over Parmesan shavings to serve.

Caesar salad with a lower fat dressing

Wild rice and basmati salad with smoked ham

perfect for a picnic lunch

Serves 4

To cook the hocks:

2 smoked ham hocks, about 1¾lb (800g) each, soaked overnight and drained

1 onion, peeled and halved

1 large carrot, peeled and cut into 3 chunks

1 celery stalk, trimmed and cut into 3 pieces

handful of Italian parsley sprigs

handful of thyme sprigs

1 bay leaf

½ tsp (2ml) black peppercorns

Salad:

¾ cup (150g) mixed basmati and wild rice

5oz (150g) green beans, trimmed and halved

handful of Italian parsley, roughly torn

squeeze of lemon juice, to taste

3 tbsp (45ml) extra-virgin olive oil

freshly ground black pepper

Put the ham hocks into a large pan with the onion, carrot, celery, herbs, and peppercorns. Pour over enough cold water to cover the hocks and bring to a boil, then skim off any scum from the surface. Cover and simmer gently for 3 to 4 hours until the hocks are very tender— the meat should slide easily from the bone.

Let the hocks cool slightly in the poaching stock, then lift onto a plate. While still warm, peel off the skin and remove the fat. Break the meat into flakes and place in a salad bowl.

Measure 4 cups (1 liter) of the ham poaching stock. (You can save the rest to make a soup.) Pour the measured stock into a medium pan and add the basmati and wild rice. Bring to a boil, lower the heat to a simmer, and cook for 20 to 25 minutes until the rice is tender.

Blanch the green beans in the meantime. Add them to a pan of boiling salted water and cook for 3 to 4 minutes until just tender. Drain and refresh under cold running water. Drain thoroughly.

When ready, drain the rice in a colander set over another pan. Place the pan lid over the colander to let the rice steam and dry out a little, then tip into the bowl containing the ham. Add the beans, parsley, lemon juice, olive oil, and a generous grinding of black pepper. Toss well and serve warm, or at room temperature if you prefer.

49

Sweet potato frittata with tomato salsa

Serves 2

1 large sweet potato, about 7–8oz (200–250g)

1 tbsp (15ml) olive oil

1 shallot, peeled and minced

sea salt and black pepper

4 large eggs

small handful of chives, finely snipped

Tomato salsa:

8oz (250g) vine-ripened plum tomatoes

2 green onions, trimmed and thinly sliced on the diagonal

handful of cilantro leaves, chopped

juice of ½ lemon

3 tbsp (45ml) extra-virgin olive oil

1 tbsp (15ml) sesame oil

dash of Tabasco sauce

pinch of sugar (optional)

To make the salsa, halve or quarter the tomatoes and place in a large bowl. Add all the other ingredients and mix well, seasoning to taste with salt and pepper, and a pinch of sugar if you like. Set aside.

For the frittata, heat the broiler to its highest setting. Peel the sweet potato and cut into ½-inch (1cm) cubes. Heat a nonstick omelet pan or skillet (suitable for use under the broiler) and add the olive oil. When hot, toss in the potato and shallot, and season well with salt and pepper. Cook over medium heat, turning occasionally, for about 4 to 5 minutes until the potatoes are just tender and lightly golden at the edges.

Lightly beat the eggs in a bowl, add the chives, and pour over the sweet potatoes. Shake the pan gently to distribute the ingredients and cook over low heat, without stirring, for a few minutes until the eggs are beginning to set at the bottom and around the sides.

Place the pan under the hot broiler briefly until the top of the frittata has set. Try not to overcook the eggs or they will turn rubbery. Let stand for a minute, then run a heatproof plastic spatula around the sides of the pan and invert the frittata onto a large plate. Spoon the tomato salsa into a neat pile on top and serve immediately.

Spinach and goat cheese soufflé

Heat the oven to 400°F (200°C). Brush 8 ramekins, 5oz (150ml) capacity, with very soft butter, using upward strokes. Set them on a baking sheet, chill for 15 minutes, then repeat with another coating of butter.

Set a large pan over medium-high heat. When hot, add the spinach and some seasoning. Stir for a few minutes until the leaves have wilted, adding a tiny splash of water as necessary. Tip into a colander set over a large bowl. Cool slightly, then wrap the spinach in a clean dish towel and squeeze out the excess moisture. Mince and set aside.

Heat the olive oil in a medium pan and add the shallot and garlic. Stir over medium heat for 4 to 6 minutes until soft. Add the flour and cayenne pepper and stir over low heat for 3 to 4 minutes. Gradually whisk in the milk. Simmer and stir for a few more minutes until the mixture becomes thick. Transfer to a large bowl and cool slightly.

Crumble the goat cheese into the mixture, then add the Parmesan and a little seasoning and stir to combine. Mix in the chopped spinach and egg yolks. Set aside.

Beat the egg whites in a clean bowl with an electric whisk to firm peaks, then fold into the spinach and cheese mixture until just combined. Spoon into the prepared ramekins and tap gently on the counter to get rid of any large air pockets. Run the tip of a small knife around the edge of each one. Bake for 13 to 15 minutes until risen and golden brown on top. Serve immediately, with a simple side salad.

Serves 8

softened butter, to grease the dishes

1lb (500g) baby leaf spinach, washed

sea salt and black pepper

3 tbsp (45ml) olive oil (or butter)

1 banana shallot, peeled and minced

2 garlic cloves, peeled and finely crushed

¼ cup (40g) all-purpose flour

pinch of cayenne pepper, or to taste

1 cup (250ml) low-fat milk

7oz (200g) soft goat cheese

2 tbsp (30ml) finely grated Parmesan

4 large eggs, separated

Spaghetti vongole

low in fat and a good source of minerals

Serves 4

4lb (2kg) fresh palourdes (carpet shell clams) in the shell

sea salt and black pepper

10oz (300g) dried spaghetti or linguine

2 tbsp (30ml) olive oil

3 fat garlic cloves, peeled

1 banana shallot, peeled and roughly sliced

1 small red chile, quartered lengthwise

handful of basil stalks

⅓ cup (75ml) dry white wine

2 tbsp (30ml) Italian parsley, minced

Scrub the clams under cold running water and discard any that do not close tightly when gently tapped on the counter. Meanwhile, bring a large pan of salted water to a boil for the pasta. When it comes to a rolling boil, add the spaghetti and cook until al dente.

Cook the clams about 6 minutes before the pasta will be ready. Heat another large pan and add the olive oil. Tip in the clams and throw in the garlic, shallot, chile, and basil stalks. Pour in the wine and cover the pan with a tight-fitting lid. Shake the pan and let steam for 3 to 4 minutes until the clams have opened. Tip the clams into a colander set over a large clean bowl. Discard any that have not opened.

Pour the clam juices back into the pan and boil for a few minutes until thickened slightly. Throw in the parsley, then taste and adjust the seasoning. Clams are naturally salty so you may find that you only need pepper.

Drain the pasta thoroughly. Immediately add to the sauce and toss to coat. Return the clams to the pan and toss again. Divide between warm plates and serve immediately, with chunks of crusty bread to mop up the juices.

Soba noodle soup
with chicken and shiitake

light, fragrant, and low in fat, yet packed with protein

Serves 4

2 large skinless boneless chicken breasts, about 5oz (150g) each

1 tbsp (15ml) tamari or light soy sauce

2 tbsp (30ml) mirin

1 tbsp (15ml) sake

1 tbsp (15ml) sesame oil, plus extra to toss

freshly ground black pepper

6 cups (1.5 liters) chicken stock (see page 249)

1 piece of kombu (Japanese dried kelp), lightly rinsed

1¼-inch (3cm) piece of gingerroot, peeled and cut into thin sticks

2–3 tbsp (30–45ml) miso paste

7oz (200g) soba noodles (Japanese buckwheat noodles)

5oz (150g) shiitake mushrooms, stems trimmed and top scored

4 green onions, trimmed and thinly sliced on the diagonal

1 tsp (5ml) toasted sesame seeds

First, marinate the chicken. Cut the chicken breasts across the grain into thin slices. Place in a bowl and add the tamari, mirin, sake, sesame oil, and a generous grinding of pepper. Give the chicken a good stir, to ensure that every piece is coated. Cover with plastic wrap and let marinate in the refrigerator for at least 30 minutes, or preferably overnight.

For the soup base, pour the chicken stock into a medium pan and add the kombu. Bring to a simmer, cover the pan with a lid, and cook gently for 5 to 10 minutes. Remove and discard the kombu, which will have imparted a lovely savory flavor to the stock. Add the ginger and stir in the miso paste. Simmer for another 3 to 5 minutes.

When ready to serve, bring a pot of water to a boil for the noodles. Add the mushrooms to the simmering stock and cook for 2 minutes, then add the chicken strips. Cook until the chicken is just opaque throughout, about 1 to 1½ minutes. Taste and adjust the seasoning. Cover the pan with a lid and turn the heat down as low as possible.

Add the noodles to the pan of boiling water and cook until tender but still retaining a slight bite, about 3 to 4 minutes. Drain and immediately toss with a little sesame oil. Divide between warm soup bowls and sprinkle over the green onions. Ladle the hot soup over the noodles, making sure that you divide the chicken and mushrooms evenly. Sprinkle with the sesame seeds and serve at once.

five-a-day

Fruit and vegetables are good sources of vitamins, minerals, antioxidants, and dietary fiber— all important for boosting our immune systems and helping to prevent life-threatening illnesses such as cancer and coronary heart disease. They are also relatively low in calories, making them an ideal food for maintaining a healthy weight and lowering fat consumption.

"Five-a-day" is the recommended intake; i.e. five portions of fruit and veg in total, not five of each. This might still seem a lot, but including plenty of fruit and vegetables in your diet is easier than you think, especially as dried, preserved, canned, and frozen ones count. That said, from a nutritional angle, fresh fruit and vegetables, dried fruit, and frozen foods— like peas that have been processed soon after picking—are generally the best choices.

A portion can simply be a piece of fruit, such as an apple, peach, or a banana, a handful of grapes or dried apricots, a glass of fruit juice, a side salad or 3½oz (100g) cooked vegetables. The easiest way to meet the "five-a-day" target is to make sure that you have at least one portion of fruit at breakfast and two portions of vegetables/fruit as part of your other meals. Raw or cooked vegetables should take up at least a third of a dinner plate. And fruit is an obvious choice for dessert, or to eat as a snack in between meals.

Vary the color of the fruits and vegetables you eat to increase the health benefits. Different antioxidants and micronutrients are associated with different colors, so to get a good balance, you need to diversify your diet and aim for a colorful plate!

Healthy working lunch

Borscht

wonderfully nutritious soup that can be eaten hot or cold

Serves 4

2 tbsp (30ml) olive oil

1 onion, peeled and minced

2 celery stalks, trimmed and minced

1 large carrot, peeled and minced

1 thyme sprig, leaves stripped

sea salt and black pepper

1lb (500g) raw beet, peeled and chopped

¼ red cabbage, about 8oz (250g), minced

3⅓ cups (800ml) vegetable stock (see page 248) or water

1 tbsp (15ml) red wine vinegar, to taste

1 tsp (5ml) superfine sugar, to taste

handful of dill, chopped

4 tbsp sour cream, or plain yogurt, to serve (optional)

Heat the olive oil in a large pan and add the onion, celery, carrot, thyme leaves, and some seasoning. Cook over medium heat, stirring frequently, for 8 to 10 minutes.

Add the beet and cabbage with a small splash of water. Stir well, then cover and cook for 10 to 12 minutes until the vegetables are just tender. Lift the lid and give the mixture a stir several times during cooking to stop the vegetables catching and burning on the bottom of the pan.

Remove the lid and pour in the stock or water to cover the vegetables. Add the wine vinegar, bring to a boil, then reduce the heat to a simmer. Cook for another 5 to 10 minutes until the vegetables are soft. Skim off any froth from the surface. Adjust the seasoning to taste with salt, pepper, and sugar.

Purée the soup with a stick blender until smooth and creamy, or leave it chunky for a traditional, rustic finish. If you decide to purée the soup, you may need to thin it down slightly with a little boiling water.

Ladle into warm bowls if serving hot; otherwise let cool, then chill thoroughly. Serve topped with the chopped dill and a spoonful of sour cream.

Chilled watercress
and spinach soup

Serves 4

2 tbsp (30ml) olive oil

1 sweet onion, peeled and minced

1 small potato, about 5oz (150g), peeled and diced

10oz (300g) watercress, washed and thicker stalks removed

2³⁄₄–3¹⁄₂oz (75–100g) baby spinach leaves, plus a handful to garnish

3¹⁄₃ cups (800ml) vegetable or chicken stock (see pages 248–9)

sea salt and black pepper

squeeze of lemon juice

3–4 tbsp (45–60ml) crème fraîche, to serve (optional)

Heat the olive oil in a large pan and add the onion and potato. Sauté gently, stirring frequently, for about 10 minutes until the vegetables are soft but not brown.

Add the watercress and spinach, then pour in enough stock to cover the vegetables. Bring to a boil and season to taste with salt, pepper, and a squeeze of lemon juice. As soon as the spinach and watercress have wilted, remove the pan from the heat.

Purée the soup in two batches, using a blender. Pour into a wide bowl and let cool completely. Cover with plastic wrap and chill for a few hours or overnight.

To serve, pour the soup into chilled bowls and garnish with a few baby spinach leaves. Add a small spoonful of crème fraîche if you wish, and grind over some pepper.

brimming with nutrients, especially vitamin C, iron, and calcium

high in fiber and healthy carbs, yet low in fat

Cranberry bean minestrone

Serves 4

2 tbsp (30ml) olive oil, plus a little extra to drizzle (optional)

2 onions, peeled and chopped

2 medium carrots, peeled and chopped

1 celery stalk, trimmed and chopped

sea salt and black pepper

few thyme sprigs

1 bay leaf

2³/₄oz (80g) smoked back (Canadian) bacon, trimmed of fat and chopped

2 tbsp (30ml) tomato paste

2 x 14oz (398g) cans cranberry beans, rinsed and drained

5oz (150g) cherry tomatoes, halved

2½–3⅓ cups (600–800ml) chicken stock (see page 249) or water

2³/₄oz (75g) spaghetti, broken into small pieces

large handful of basil, finely shredded

Parmesan, for grating (optional)

Heat the olive oil in a large pan and add the onions, carrots, celery, and some seasoning. Stir frequently over medium-high heat for 6 to 8 minutes until the vegetables are beginning to soften. Add the thyme, bay leaf, and bacon. Increase the heat slightly and cook, stirring, for another 2 minutes. Stir in the tomato paste and cook for another minute.

Tip in the cranberry beans and cherry tomatoes, then pour in the chicken stock or water to cover. Bring to a gentle simmer. Add the spaghetti and cook for 10 minutes. Taste and adjust the seasoning.

To serve, ladle into warm soup bowls and sprinkle over the shredded basil. If you wish, add a restrained drizzle of olive oil, and grate a little Parmesan over each portion. Serve with chunks of rustic country bread.

Spiced lentil soup

lentils are digested slowly, leaving you feeling full for longer

Serves 4

generous 1⅓ cups (275g) split red lentils

2 tbsp (30ml) olive oil

1 large onion, peeled and minced

2 large garlic cloves, peeled and minced

1 tsp (5ml) ground cumin

1 tsp (5ml) ground coriander

2 tsp (10ml) garam masala

½ tsp (2ml) ground ginger

½ tsp (2ml) ground turmeric

1 tbsp (15ml) tomato paste

3⅓ cups (800ml) vegetable or chicken stock (see pages 248–9)

To finish:

1 tbsp (15ml) olive oil (optional)

1 tsp (5ml) mustard seeds (optional)

1 tsp (5ml) kalonji (black onion) seeds (optional)

3–4 tbsp (45–60ml) plain yogurt

cilantro leaves

Rinse the lentils in a colander and drain well. Heat the olive oil in a medium pan and add the onion and garlic. Sauté for 4 to 6 minutes until lightly golden. Stir in the ground spices and tomato paste and cook for another 2 minutes.

Tip in the lentils and pour in the stock to cover. Bring to a boil, then reduce the heat. Simmer, uncovered, for 25 to 30 minutes or until the lentils are very soft, giving them a stir every now and then. You may need to top off with a little more water toward the end of cooking if the soup seems too thick. Taste and adjust the seasoning.

Ladle half of the soup into a blender and whiz to a purée, then pour back into the pan. The soup should be somewhat chunky. Adjust the consistency again if necessary, adding a little boiling water to thin it down.

For a little extra spice and fragrance if required, heat the 1 tbsp (15ml) olive oil in a small pan and tip in the mustard and black onion seeds. When they begin to pop, pour the mixture over the soup and stir.

Ladle the soup into warm bowls and top with a spoonful of yogurt and a few cilantro leaves. Serve with warm Indian bread on the side.

Tabbouleh with goat cheese

a range of vital nutrients and lots of fiber

Serves 4

1 cup (150g) bulgur wheat

sea salt and black pepper

4 green onions

3 ripe plum tomatoes

bunch of Italian parsley, chopped

bunch of mint, chopped

finely grated rind of 1 lemon

2 tbsp (30ml) lemon juice

2 tbsp (30ml) extra-virgin olive oil, plus extra to drizzle (optional)

pinch of superfine sugar (optional)

5oz (150g) soft goat cheese

Put the bulgur wheat into a pan and pour on enough water to cover by 1¼–1½ inches (3–4cm). Add some seasoning and bring to a boil, then reduce the heat slightly. Simmer for about 12 to 15 minutes until the bulgur wheat is tender but still retains a bite.

In the meantime, trim and finely slice the green onions on the diagonal. Halve, seed, and mince the tomatoes and place in a salad bowl with the green onions. Trim the herb bunches, discarding the thicker stalks, then chop them fairly finely and add to the bowl.

When it is ready, drain the bulgur wheat in a colander or strainer and let dry out for a few minutes. Tip into the salad bowl, then add the lemon rind and juice, olive oil, sugar if required, and seasoning to taste. Toss to mix. Crumble over the goat cheese, and drizzle over a little olive oil if you wish.

Note If you're preparing this salad for a packed lunch, let the bulgur wheat cool completely before tossing with the herbs, tomatoes, and onions.

Rice noodle salad
with shrimp and Thai dressing

Serves 2–3

3½oz (100g) thin rice noodles

drizzle of sesame oil

7oz (200g) snow peas or sugar snap peas

1 large sweet red pepper

1 large sweet yellow or orange pepper

2 green onions

7oz (200g) peeled, cooked shrimp

handful of cilantro leaves

1 tbsp (15ml) toasted black or white sesame seeds, to sprinkle

Dressing:

1 shallot, peeled and finely diced

2 garlic cloves, peeled and finely crushed

1 small red chile, seeded and minced

2–3 tbsp (30–45ml) lime juice, or more to taste

2 tbsp (30ml) fish sauce

1 tbsp (15ml) light soy sauce

2½ tbsp (38ml) jaggery (or soft brown sugar)

2 tbsp (30ml) toasted sesame oil

Bring the kettle to a boil. Place the rice noodles in a large heatproof bowl and pour on boiling water, ensuring that the noodles are fully immersed. Cover the bowl with plastic wrap and let stand for 5 minutes or until the noodles are tender but still retaining a bite. Drain and immediately toss with a drizzle of sesame oil to stop them sticking to each other.

In the meantime, blanch the snow peas in a pan of boiling water for 2 minutes until they are just tender but still bright green. Refresh in a bowl of iced water, then drain well. Cut the snow peas on the diagonal into 2 or 3 pieces. Halve, core, and seed the peppers, then cut into long, thin slices. Trim and finely slice the green onions on the diagonal.

For the dressing, put all the ingredients into a bowl and whisk lightly to combine.

Put the shrimp, green onions, snow peas, and peppers into a large bowl and add the drained noodles, cilantro leaves, and sesame seeds. Pour the dressing over the salad and toss well to coat. Eat immediately or chill until ready to serve.

Note If you're preparing this salad for a packed lunch, let the noodles cool completely before tossing with the other ingredients.

Flatbread, feta, and chickpea salad

tasty, nutritious, and sustaining

Serves 3–4

2 large, thin flatbreads or pita breads

½ tsp (2ml) paprika

4 tbsp (60ml) olive oil

1 red onion, peeled and thinly sliced

2 garlic cloves, peeled and thinly sliced

½ red chile, seeded and minced

14oz (398g) can chickpeas, rinsed and drained

generous squeeze of lemon juice

large handful of Italian parsley leaves

sea salt and black pepper

5oz (150g) feta cheese

Heat the oven to 350°F (180°C). Split the breads horizontally. Mix the paprika with 2 tbsp (30ml) of the olive oil. Brush each piece of bread with this mixture and place on a baking sheet. Bake until lightly golden brown and crisp, just 2 to 3 minutes for thin atbreads, 4 to 5 minutes for pita bread.

Meanwhile, heat the remaining olive oil in a pan, add the onion, and cook, stirring, over medium heat for 6 to 8 minutes until soft. Add the garlic and chile and sauté for another minute. Tip in the chickpeas and stir to mix. Squeeze over the lemon juice and add the parsley and a little seasoning to taste.

Warm the chickpeas through, then tip into a large bowl and let stand for a few minutes. Crumble over two-thirds of the cheese and toss well. Divide between serving plates and crumble over the remaining feta. Break the bread into smaller pieces and serve on the side.

Note If you're preparing this salad for a packed lunch, let the chickpea mixture cool completely before adding the feta. Pack the bread in a separate airtight container to keep it crisp.

Creole spiced bean
and vegetable salad

high in fiber, low in fat, and plenty of slow-release energy

2 tbsp (30ml) olive oil

1 onion, peeled and thinly sliced

sea salt and black pepper

7oz (200g) green beans, trimmed

2 zucchini, trimmed and sliced into
⅝-inch (1.5cm) circles

8 green onions, trimmed and cut into
short lengths

14oz (398g) can haricot or lima beans,
rinsed and drained

14oz (398g) can cannellini beans, rinsed
and drained

14oz (398g) can chickpeas, rinsed and
drained

8oz (250g) cherry tomatoes, halved

bunch of Italian parsley, leaves only,
roughly chopped

bunch of cilantro, leaves only,
roughly chopped

Creole spice mix:

1½ tsp (7ml) sweet paprika

1½ tsp (7ml) dried basil

1½ tsp (7ml) dried thyme

pinch of cayenne pepper, or to taste

pinch of chili powder, or to taste

Heat the olive oil in a pan and add the onion with some salt and pepper. Stir frequently over medium heat for 6 to 8 minutes until the onion is soft.

Meanwhile, combine the ingredients for the Creole spice mix in a small bowl. Add to the pan and stir for another minute or two until fragrant.

Tip the green beans, zucchini, and green onions into the pan and cook for 6 to 8 minutes until tender. Turn off the heat, add the canned beans and chickpeas along with the cherry tomatoes, and toss to mix.

Transfer the salad to a large bowl and stir in the chopped parsley and cilantro. Serve slightly warm or at room temperature.

5 ways with
oily fish

Sardines, mackerel, tuna, and other oily fish are rich in omega-3 fatty acids. These essential nutrients offer a range of benefits —not least for a healthy brain, eyes, and skin. Growing up, I used to cringe at the thought of swallowing a spoonful of cod liver oil … little did I know then that oily fish are a much better source of omega-3's. The fish must, however, be fresh— canned tuna, sardines, etc., won't give you the same benefits because most of those omega-3's are lost in the canning process. Not only are oily fish like mackerel, pilchards, and sardines healthy, they are also abundant—and some of the cheapest fish available. We really should be eating more of them.

1

Escabeche of mackerel

Season 4 filleted, pin-boned mackerel and lay in a lightly oiled wide dish. Heat 2–3 tbsp (30–45ml) olive oil in a pan and add 1 finely sliced large carrot, 1 finely sliced banana shallot, 2 star anise, a pinch of saffron strands, ½ tsp (2ml) crushed coriander seeds, and a pinch of salt. Pan-fry for 2 to 3 minutes, then add ¼ cup (50ml) white wine vinegar, ⅔ cup (150ml) dry white wine, and 1 tbsp (15ml) superfine sugar. Simmer for 5 minutes, then adjust the seasoning. Pour the hot marinade over the fish and cool. Cover with plastic wrap and chill overnight.

Serve at room temperature, sprinkled with chopped cilantro leaves, with crusty bread on the side. The mackerel is best eaten without the skin. **Serves 4**

2

Smoked mackerel and fennel salad

Shave 2 large fennel bulbs, using a mandolin. Immerse in iced water for 10 minutes to crisp up. Drain well and tip into a salad bowl. Flake 2 peppered smoked mackerel fillets (about 5½oz/160g) and add to the fennel. For the dressing, whisk together 4 tsp (20ml) grainy mustard, 4 tsp (20ml) runny honey, 4 tsp (20ml) lemon juice, 6–7 tbsp (90–105ml) extra-virgin olive oil, and some seasoning. Add a handful of chopped dill to the fennel with the dressing and toss well. **Serves 4**

3 Herrings with mustard and dill

For the sauce, peel and seed 1 small cucumber, then grate and squeeze out the excess water. Mix with a handful of chopped dill, generous ¾ cup (200ml) plain yogurt, the juice of ½ lemon, salt, pepper, and a pinch of paprika.

Fillet 4 cleaned whole herrings (about 8oz/250g each) and check for pinbones, then brush 2 tbsp (30ml) mustard over the boned sides. Mix 4–5 tbsp (60–75g) rolled oats with 1 tsp (5ml) thyme leaves and use to coat the herring fillets. Heat 1–2 tbsp (15–30ml) olive oil in a nonstick skillet and pan-fry the fish for about a minute on each side. Serve immediately, with the sauce. **Serves 4**

4 Seared tuna with Swiss chard

Season 4 tuna steaks, each 5oz (150g) and ¾ inches (2cm) thick. Sprinkle with chopped cilantro, drizzle over a little olive oil, and let marinate for 10 minutes. Separate the leaves and stalks of a large bunch of Swiss chard. Thinly slice the stalks and roughly chop the leaves. Heat a little olive oil in a large pan and lightly sauté 2 minced garlic cloves and 1 minced seeded red chile. Add the chard stalks, some seasoning, and a little splash of water. Cover and cook for 5 minutes. Tip in the leaves and cook for another 3 to 5 minutes until tender. Season the tuna steaks and sear in a nonstick skillet for 1 to 1½ minutes each side. Rest for a few minutes, then serve with the chard. **Serves 4**

5 Tomato and olive crusted trout fillets

Heat oven to 400°F (200°C). Lightly season 4 skinless trout fillets, about 4½oz (130g) each, and place on a lightly oiled baking sheet, skinned side up. For the crust, in a bowl, mix 2 cups (100g) fresh bread crumbs with 1 crushed garlic clove, 1oz (30g) chopped sun-dried tomatoes, ¼ cup (30ml) chopped pitted black olives, and 1–2 tbsp (15–30ml) olive oil. Roughly chop a handful of basil leaves and add to the bowl. Toss to mix and season to taste. Spread the crust over each trout fillet, patting down lightly with the back of the spoon. Bake for 10 to 12 minutes until the crust is golden and crisp. Serve at once, with minted new potatoes if you wish. **Serves 4**

Glazed salmon
with spinach and radish salad

4 lightly smoked salmon fillets,
4–5oz (125–150g) each

3½oz (100g) baby spinach leaves, washed
and dried

8–10 radishes, washed, trimmed, and
finely sliced

Marinade:

3 tbsp (45ml) honey

1 tbsp (15ml) lemon juice

2 tbsp (30ml) light soy sauce

1 tsp (5ml) Dijon mustard

½ tsp (2ml) grated gingerroot

Dressing:

1 tbsp (15ml) grated gingerroot

3 tbsp (45ml) rice wine vinegar

2 tbsp (30ml) light soy sauce

2 tbsp (30ml) sesame oil

2–3 tbsp (30–45ml) tahini (sesame
seed paste)

Remove the skin from the salmon and check carefully for pin-bones, pulling out any with kitchen tweezers. Place the fillets side by side in a shallow dish. For the marinade, mix the ingredients together in a bowl, then pour over the salmon to coat. Cover with plastic wrap and let marinate in the refrigerator for 30 minutes to allow the flavors to permeate.

For the dressing, whisk together all the ingredients in a bowl and set aside.

Heat the oven to 450°F (230°C). Arrange the spinach leaves on individual plates and top with the radish slices.

Lift the salmon from the marinade and arrange on a lightly oiled baking sheet. Cook in the oven for 4 to 6 minutes until medium rare, basting after 2 minutes. The fish should feel slightly springy when pressed.

Place a salmon fillet in the middle of each plate and drizzle the ginger and tahini dressing over the salad to serve.

Note If you're preparing this salad for a packed lunch, let the salmon cool and pack the dressing and salad leaves in separate containers. Assemble just before eating.

packed with essential nutrients

Mango, avocado, and smoked chicken salad

Serves 4

2 medium, firm but ripe mangoes

2 ripe avocados

squeeze of lemon juice

10oz–²/₃lb (300–350g) smoked chicken breasts

7oz (200g) mixed salad leaves, such as arugula, mâche (lamb's lettuce), baby chard, or amaranth

2 tbsp (30ml) pine nuts, toasted (optional)

Dressing:

2 tbsp (30ml) orange juice

2 tbsp (30ml) lemon juice

1 tbsp (15ml) whole grain mustard

2 tbsp (30ml) extra-virgin olive oil

2 tbsp (30ml) avocado oil (or olive oil)

sea salt and black pepper

Peel the mangoes and cut the flesh away from the seed into thin slices. Arrange on four serving plates.

Halve the avocados and remove the pit. Peel off the skin and slice the flesh into strips. Squeeze over a little lemon juice to stop the flesh discoloring, then arrange over the mango slices.

Cut the chicken into thin slices and divide between the plates. Neatly pile the salad leaves in the middle.

For the dressing, whisk the ingredients together in a bowl, seasoning with salt and pepper to taste. Spoon the dressing over the salad and serve, topped with a handful of toasted pine nuts if you like.

Note If you're preparing this salad for a packed lunch, pack the dressing and salad in separate containers and combine just before eating.

healthy snacks

Snacking gives you an energy boost, which you may need—even between healthy meals—if you're very active. It's what you eat that makes a difference. So, ditch the bag of potato chips and make healthy choices to curb hunger pangs:

Dried fruits and nuts These are concentrated sources of many nutrients. Dried apricots, for example, are high in fiber, vitamins, and minerals. Nuts are a good source of protein and minerals; walnuts, in particular, are rich in essential fats.

Healthy dips Swap fattening potato chips for vegetable sticks and serve with homemade dips so that you can control the amount of oil added. Avocados are great for making guacamole and they're rich in good fats, vitamins, and minerals.

Low-fat yogurts Choose from cow's, sheep, or goat milk yogurts, which are loaded with calcium but without the excess fat and calories. Eat with a drizzle of natural honey or some dried fruit compote.

Oats Whether they come in the form of oatcakes, muffins, biscuits, or cereal bars, oats are the perfect food for snacking on, because they release energy slowly as the body takes time to digest them. Just be mindful of the high amount of sugar and fat in most commercially produced cereal bars and bakes.

Smoothies Make your own using bananas, reduced-fat yogurt and virtually any tangy fruit you fancy. Smoothies keep you feeling full for longer, too.

Chocolate Yes, eating too much will make your thighs bigger but a little good quality dark chocolate is a useful source of antioxidants. A few squares (not the whole bar) will suffice.

Fresh fruit "An apple a day keeps the doctor away ..."

Healthy Sunday lunch

Baked sea bass
with lemon couscous

healthy white fish—low in fat, high in protein and B vitamins

Serves 4

1 sea bass, about 2lb (1.1kg), scaled and cleaned

sea salt and black pepper

olive oil, to drizzle

few rosemary sprigs

handful of large basil leaves

2 large garlic cloves, peeled and thinly sliced

½ lemon, cut into wedges

Couscous:

1¼ cups (250g) couscous

finely grated rind of 1 lemon

1 tender rosemary sprig, leaves stripped and minced

1¼ cups (300ml) boiling water or chicken stock (see page 249)

2½ cups (250g) peas, thawed if frozen

juice of ½ lemon

4 tbsp extra-virgin olive oil

bunch of Italian parsley, chopped

Heat the oven to 400°F (200°C). Score the sea bass on both sides and rub all over with salt, pepper, and a little drizzle of olive oil. Pick the rosemary sprigs off the hard stems. Roll a large basil leaf tightly around each rosemary sprig. Insert into the slashes in the fish, along with the garlic slices.

Lay the sea bass on a lightly oiled foil-lined baking sheet. Stuff the cavity with the lemon wedges and remaining rosemary. Bake for 15 to 20 minutes until the flesh is opaque and just cooked through— you should be able to pull out a fin easily.

Prepare the couscous while the fish is in the oven. Put the couscous, lemon rind, rosemary, and some seasoning into a large bowl. Pour over the boiling water or stock, cover with plastic wrap, and leave for 5 minutes. Meanwhile, cook the peas in boiling water for 3 to 4 minutes until tender.

For the dressing, mix the lemon juice with the olive oil and some seasoning to taste. Once the couscous has absorbed all the liquid, fluff it up with a fork. Drain the peas and add to the couscous along with the dressing and chopped parsley. Toss to mix.

Serve the fish with the warm couscous and steamed bok choy or green beans.

Note To serve eight, cook two sea bass of this size rather than a larger fish and make double the quantity of couscous.

Marinated halibut
with spiced eggplant

Serves 4

6 skinless halibut fillets, about 4½oz (130g) each

3 tbsp (45ml) olive oil

sea salt and black pepper

¾ tsp (3ml) ground turmeric

Spiced eggplant:

3 large eggplants

5 tbsp olive oil

3 large onions, peeled and finely sliced

2 tsp (10ml) ground cumin

3 plum tomatoes, peeled, seeded, and chopped

1 cup (150g) golden raisins, soaked in hot water for 10 minutes

2–3 tbsp (30–45ml) lemon juice, to taste

handful of basil leaves, torn

Lay the fish in a shallow dish and drizzle over the olive oil. Sprinkle with pepper and the turmeric, and rub all over to coat evenly. Cover with plastic wrap and let marinate in the refrigerator for a few hours, or for at least 20 minutes.

Heat the oven to 400°F (200°C). Cut the eggplants into 1¼-inch (3cm) chunks, sprinkle with salt, and let stand in a colander set over a bowl for 20 minutes. (Doing this prevents them from absorbing as much oil during cooking.)

Rinse the eggplant to remove the salt, drain well, and pat dry with paper towels. Toss the chunks on a baking sheet with some black pepper and 2–3 tbsp (30–45ml) olive oil. Bake for 20 to 25 minutes until the eggplant chunks are soft.

Meanwhile, heat the remaining 2 tbsp (30ml) olive oil in a pan. Add the onions with some seasoning and sweat over medium heat for 8 to 10 minutes until soft. Add the cumin and cook for a few more minutes until the onions are lightly caramelized. Take off the heat. When the eggplant is ready, add to the onions with the tomatoes, golden raisins, lemon juice, and salt and pepper to taste.

To cook the fish, heat a large nonstick skillet and pan-fry the fish fillets for 2 minutes on each side—they should feel just firm when lightly pressed. Let rest for a minute or two, while you reheat the spiced eggplant. Pile it onto warm plates and top with the halibut fillets. Scatter the basil around and drizzle over a little turmeric oil from the pan.

Roast chicken
with baby vegetables

buy organic or free-range chicken for the best flavor

Serves 4–6

1 large chicken, about 4lb (1.8–2kg)

sea salt and black pepper

1 tbsp (15ml) olive oil, plus a little extra to drizzle

1 head of garlic, halved horizontally

2 lemons, halved

handful of thyme sprigs

few rosemary sprigs

10oz (300g) baby carrots, scrubbed

10oz (300g) baby turnips, washed and halved if quite large

generous 1/3 cup (100ml) dry white wine

1 1/4 cups (300ml) chicken stock (see page 249)

Heat the oven to 450°F (230°C). Rub the chicken all over with salt, pepper, and a little drizzle of olive oil. Place in a large roasting pan and stuff the cavity with half the head of garlic, 2 or 3 lemon halves, and a few herb sprigs.

Roast the chicken for 20 minutes, then take it out of the oven and lower the setting to 400°F (200°C). Add the carrots and turnips to the roasting pan and turn to baste in the juices. Put the remaining garlic, lemon halves, and herbs around the chicken. Drizzle a little olive oil over the bird and vegetables, and sprinkle with a little salt and pepper. Roast for another 35 to 40 minutes or until the bird is golden brown and cooked through—the juices should run clear when the thickest part of the thigh is pierced with a knife.

When ready, lift the chicken onto a warm platter, cover with foil, and let rest for 10 to 15 minutes in a warm place. Put the vegetables into a warm dish, cover, and keep hot.

Meanwhile, skim off any fat from the cooking juices in the roasting pan, then place on the stove over medium heat. Add the wine, scraping up the sediment from the bottom of the pan to deglaze and let bubble until reduced by half. Pour in the stock and again boil until reduced by half. Add any juices from the rested chicken, then strain into a warm pitcher.

Carve the chicken and divide the meat and roasted vegetables between warm plates. Pour the sauce over the chicken. Serve with new potatoes and a green vegetable, such as broccoli or Brussels sprouts.

Sticky baked chicken drumsticks

Serves 5

olive oil, to drizzle

10 chicken drumsticks

sea salt and black pepper

Glaze:

6 tbsp (90ml) honey

3 tbsp (45ml) fish sauce

4 tsp (20ml) light soy sauce

juice of 1½ lemons

3 tbsp (45ml) rice wine vinegar

4 tsp (20ml) sesame oil

Heat the oven to 400°F (200°C). Lightly oil a large baking dish. Season the drumsticks with salt and pepper and arrange in the dish in a single layer. Drizzle over a little olive oil and bake in the hot oven for 20 minutes.

Prepare the glaze in the meantime. Mix all the ingredients together in a small bowl until evenly combined.

Take the chicken out of the oven and pour over the glaze, to coat each drumstick. Return to the oven and bake for another 20 to 30 minutes, turning several times, until the chicken is tender and nicely glazed.

Let the chicken rest for a few minutes before serving. For a balanced meal, serve with steamed rice and purple sprouting broccoli or green beans.

Pheasant and ginger casserole

low in fat and cholesterol, pheasant is a healthy choice

Serves 4

2 oven-ready pheasants, about 1½lb (750g) each

sea salt and black pepper

2 large carrots, peeled and each cut into 3 chunks

2 large celery stalks, trimmed and each cut into 3 pieces

7oz (200g) cipollini or pearl onions, peeled

2 x 2-inch (5cm) pieces of gingerroot, halved lengthwise

1 head of garlic, halved horizontally

handful of thyme sprigs

few rosemary sprigs

5 cloves

2 star anise (optional)

1 tsp (5ml) black peppercorns

Rub the pheasants all over with a little salt and pepper and lay them breast side down in a large cast-iron pan or other ovenproof casserole. Add the carrots, celery, and onions, along with the ginger, garlic, herbs, cloves, star anise if using, and peppercorns. Pour in enough water to come two-thirds of the way up the sides of the pheasants.

Place over high heat and bring to a boil. Immediately lower the heat to a simmer, partially cover the pan with a lid, and cook gently for 35 to 40 minutes until the pheasants are tender, turning them over halfway through cooking.

To serve, lift the pheasants out of the broth and either carve them into smaller joints or remove the meat from the carcass and break into shreds. Divide between warm bowls and ladle over the hot broth and vegetables. Serve with chunks of rustic bread.

Roasted filet of beef with tomato tarragon dressing

red meat is an excellent source of protein and iron

Serves 6

2²/₃lb (1.2kg) prime beef filet (in one piece, cut from the thick end)

sea salt and black pepper

2 tbsp (30ml) olive oil

few handfuls of wild arugula leaves

Tomato tarragon dressing:

about 6 (1lb/500g) ripe plum tomatoes

5 tbsp (75ml) homemade ketchup (see page 125)

2 tbsp (30ml) Worcestershire sauce

1 tbsp (15ml) Dijon mustard

few dashes of Tabasco sauce

juice of 1 lemon

2 tbsp (30ml) balsamic vinegar

2 tbsp (30ml) extra-virgin olive oil

2 shallots, peeled and minced

large handful each of tarragon and Italian parsley, chopped

To make the dressing, cut each tomato in half and squeeze out the seeds. Mince the flesh and place in a large bowl. Add the rest of the ingredients except for the herbs, and mix well. Season well with salt and pepper to taste. Cover with plastic wrap and chill for at least 20 minutes or until ready to serve.

Heat the oven to 400°F (200°C) and preheat a roasting pan. Trim any fat or sinew from the filet of beef and season all over with salt and pepper. Heat a nonstick skillet with a little olive oil. When it is very hot, add the beef and sear for 1½ to 2 minutes on each side until evenly browned all over. Lightly oil the hot roasting pan.

Transfer the beef to the roasting pan and place in the oven. Roast for 25 minutes for medium rare beef—it should feel a little springy when lightly pressed. Transfer the filet to a warm platter and let rest for 10 minutes.

Serve the beef warm or at room temperature. Slice it thickly and overlap the slices on a serving platter. Pile the arugula into the center. Stir the chopped herbs into the tomato tarragon dressing and spoon over the beef. Accompany with new potatoes if you like.

Spicy beef curry

Serves 8–10

4lb (2kg) good quality lean braising beef or chuck steak

sea salt and black pepper

4 tsp (20ml) garam masala

4 tbsp (60ml) plain yogurt

4–5 tbsp (60–75ml) light olive oil

4 large sweet onions, peeled and minced

4 garlic cloves, peeled and minced

2-inch (5cm) piece of gingerroot, peeled and finely grated

4 tbsp (60ml) tomato paste

2 tbsp (30ml) superfine sugar, or to taste

2 x 14oz (398g) cans chopped tomatoes

3⅓ cups (800ml) beef stock (see page 249)

small handful of cilantro, leaves separated, stalks minced

6–8 cardamom pods

15–20 curry leaves

6 long green chiles

Spice mix:

4 tsp (20ml) coriander seeds

4 tsp (20ml) cumin seeds

1 tsp (5ml) fennel seeds

1 tsp (5ml) fenugreek seeds (optional)

4 tsp (20ml) mild curry powder

1 tsp (5ml) ground turmeric

Cut the beef into bite-size chunks, put into a bowl, and season with salt and pepper. Sprinkle with the garam masala, add the yogurt, and toss to coat. Cover with plastic wrap and let marinate in the refrigerator for at least 30 minutes, or overnight. Remove and set aside before you start to prepare the curry.

For the spice mix, toast the coriander, cumin, fennel, and fenugreek if using, in a dry pan, tossing over high heat for a few minutes until the seeds are fragrant. Tip into a mortar, add a pinch of salt, and grind to a fine powder. Stir in the curry powder and turmeric.

Heat a thin film of olive oil in a large cast-iron casserole or a heavy pan. Add the onions, garlic, ginger, and a little salt and pepper. Stir, then cover and cook for 8 to 10 minutes until the onions are soft, lifting the lid to give the mixture a stir a few times.

Add a little more oil, tip in the ground spice mix, and cook, stirring, for 2 minutes. Add the tomato paste and sugar and stir over medium-high heat for a few minutes until the onions are lightly caramelized. Add the tomatoes, beef stock, coriander stalks, cardamom pods, curry leaves, and green chiles.

Add the beef and stir until well coated in the sauce, then partially cover the pan with a lid. Simmer very gently, stirring occasionally for 3 to 4 hours, depending on the cut of beef, until the meat is meltingly tender.

To serve, ladle the curry into warm bowls and sprinkle over the cilantro leaves. Accompany with a steaming bowl of basmati rice or warmed Indian bread.

Venison pie with sweet potato topping

Serves 4–5

1⅓lb (600g) haunch of venison

sea salt and black pepper

3 tbsp (45ml) all-purpose flour

3–4 tbsp (45–60ml) olive oil

2 leeks, white part only, sliced thickly

5oz (150g) pearl onions, peeled

8oz (250g) small carrots, scrubbed

8oz (250g) crimini mushrooms, halved

1 large rosemary sprig, leaves only

⅔ cup (150ml) red wine or port

2¾ cups (650ml) chicken stock (see page 249)

5oz (150g) new potatoes, scrubbed

Sweet potato topping:

1lb (500g) sweet potatoes

⅔lb (350g) waxy potatoes

4 tsp (20ml) butter

1½oz (50g) double Gloucester cheese, shredded

2 large egg yolks

Cut the venison into 1¼-inch (3cm) chunks. Season the flour and use to coat the venison. Heat 2 tbsp (30ml) oil in a large ovenproof casserole and brown the meat in batches until evenly browned, about 2 minutes each side. Transfer to a bowl.

Add the leeks, onions, and carrots to the casserole with a little more oil and stir over medium heat for 4 to 5 minutes until colored. Add the mushrooms and rosemary and cook for a minute. Pour in the wine, scraping the bottom of the pan with a wooden spoon to deglaze. Bubble until reduced right down.

Pour in the stock and bring to a simmer. Return the venison, with any juices released, to the pan. Partially cover with a lid and gently braise for 40 to 50 minutes until the venison is tender, giving the mixture a stir every once in a while.

About 15 minutes before the venison will be ready, slice the new potatoes into ½-inch (1cm) thick circles. Season and cook in a little olive oil in a wide nonstick skillet until golden brown on both sides. Add to the casserole to finish cooking. Once the potatoes and venison are tender, remove the pan from the heat and let cool slightly.

For the topping, peel all the potatoes and cut into 2-inch (5cm) chunks. Cook in a pan of salted water for 15 minutes until tender. Drain and mash with a potato ricer back into the pan. While still hot, add the butter, cheese, and seasoning. Mix well to combine. Cool slightly, then mix in the egg yolks.

Heat the oven to 425°F (220°C). Tip the venison mixture into a large pie dish or a shallow cast-iron pan and top with the mash. Rough up the surface with a fork. Bake for 20 minutes until the topping is golden brown and the filling is bubbling around the sides. Grind over some pepper and serve.

buy prime quality
meat for optimum flavor

Roast lamb
with paprika and oranges

Serves 6–8

1 part-boned leg of lamb, about 5½lb (2.4kg), with knuckle bone left in

1 tsp (5ml) sweet paprika

1 tsp (5ml) smoked paprika

1 tsp (5ml) ground ginger

sea salt and black pepper

little drizzle of olive oil

4–5 garlic cloves, halved with skins left on

2 oranges, sliced

Heat the oven to 425°F (220°C). Trim away any excess fat from the lamb, then lightly score the surface fat in a crisscross pattern. Mix the sweet and smoked paprika with the ground ginger and a pinch each of salt and pepper. Rub all over the lamb, including the boned-out cavity, with a little olive oil. Place the lamb on a rack over a large roasting pan and stuff the boned cavity with the garlic cloves and half of the orange slices. Pour a splash of water into the pan.

Roast the lamb in the hot oven for 20 minutes, then reduce the oven setting to 375°F (190°C) and roast for another 20 minutes per 1lb (500g) for pink lamb. If during roasting the top appears to be darkening too quickly, cover with foil. About 30 minutes before you calculate the lamb will be ready, lay the remaining orange slices over the meat.

Transfer the lamb to a warm platter, cover loosely with foil, and let rest in a warm place for 10 minutes before carving.

When ready to serve, carve the lamb into thin slices and serve with new potatoes and a leafy salad.

Glazed ham
with pineapple salsa

Serves 6

1 unsmoked boned ham joint, about 6lb (2.6kg), soaked overnight

1 large carrot, peeled and cut into 3 chunks

1 large onion, peeled and halved

2 large celery stalks, cut into 3 chunks

1 bay leaf

few thyme sprigs

1 tsp (5ml) black peppercorns

about 30–40 cloves

a little oil, for oiling

3 tbsp (45ml) marmalade

1¼-inch (3cm) piece of gingerroot, peeled and finely grated

2 tbsp (30ml) light soy sauce

2–3 tbsp (30–45ml) water

Pineapple salsa:

1 large ripe pineapple

1 small cucumber

1 red chile, minced

handful of cilantro, leaves only, chopped

handful of mint, leaves only, chopped

sea salt and black pepper

1 tbsp (15ml) sesame oil

2 tbsp (30ml) olive oil

few dashes of Tabasco sauce

juice of ½ lemon

Drain the ham and place in a large cooking pot. Cover with fresh water, bring to a boil, and let bubble gently for 5 to 10 minutes. Skim off the scum and froth that rise to the surface, then pour off the water and re-cover the joint with fresh cold water. Bring to a boil, skim, then turn the heat down to a simmer and add the vegetables, herbs, and peppercorns. Simmer for about 2 hours, checking the liquid from time to time and topping off with hot water as necessary.

Lift the ham out of the pot onto a cutting board and let cool slightly. (If the liquor is not too salty, save it to make a pea and ham soup.) While still warm, cut away and discard the skin and most of the fat, leaving an even layer. Score lightly in a crisscross pattern, then stud a clove in the middle of each scored diamond.

Heat the oven to 375°F (190°C). Place the ham in a lightly oiled roasting pan. Mix together the marmalade, ginger, soy sauce, and water to make a glaze and brush all over the ham to coat evenly. Roast for 20 to 25 minutes, basting several times, until browned and nicely glazed. You may need to turn the pan around halfway through to ensure that the joint colors evenly.

Make the salsa in the meantime. Cut away the peel and "eyes" from the pineapple, then slice and remove the core. Cut the slices into ½-inch (1cm) cubes and place in a large bowl. Peel the cucumber, halve lengthwise, and scoop out the seeds, then finely dice the flesh. Add to the pineapple with all the other ingredients and mix well. Let stand for at least 20 minutes.

Rest the cooked ham, covered with foil, in a warm place for 15 minutes. Carve into thin slices and serve with the pineapple salsa and vegetables of your choice.

Avoid the bad fats

A fat-free diet isn't something I'd advocate, not only because I cannot cook without olive oil and a little butter, but because it is actually healthy to consume a small amount of fat. The idea is to eat much less of the bad stuff and a bit more of the good stuff. It certainly helps to understand what's what.

Olive oil is considered to be one of the better fats to use in cooking. Like canola, peanut, and avocado oils, it is classed as monounsaturated fat, which is effective in lowering bad cholesterol and raising good cholesterol.

Other vegetable oils, such as sunflower, corn, soy, and safflower oils, are classed as polyunsaturated oils. These are also deemed to be heart healthy if consumed in moderation. They also provide essential fatty acids, those all-important omega-3's and omega-6's, and can lower bad cholesterol.

Saturated fats are mostly found in animal products, such as red meat, butter, lard, hard cheeses, creams, and whole milk, as well as palm oil. They increase both good and bad cholesterol and should be eaten in moderation. To cut down on these fats, choose lean cuts of meat and trim off most of the fat before cooking. Use butter and cream sparingly in cooking and don't, as a matter of course, spread butter on bread—a good quality rustic loaf tastes just as good without it.

Hydrogenated oils used in processed foods, commercially baked pastries, shortenings, and certain margarines are referred to as trans fats or trans fatty acids. These fats have a devastating effect on good health because they increase bad cholesterol and lower good cholesterol. Needless to say, it's best to consume as little of these as possible.

Healthy barbecues

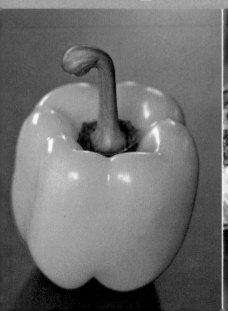

Squid with roasted peppers
and cannellini beans

Serves 4

3 large squid, about 6½oz (180g) each, cleaned, with tentacles

few thyme sprigs, leaves stripped

few rosemary sprigs, leaves stripped

½ tsp (2ml) coriander seeds, crushed

1 small red chile, sliced on the diagonal

2 garlic cloves, peeled and sliced

finely pared rind of 1 lemon

juice of 1½ lemons

3–4 tbsp (45–60ml) olive oil, to drizzle

10oz (284g) jar roasted peppers, drained

2 x 14oz (398g) cans cannellini beans, rinsed and drained

sea salt and black pepper

small bunch of Italian parsley, chopped

To prepare the squid, cut along one side of the body pouches to open them out, then lightly score the flesh in a crisscross pattern. Lay the scored squid and tentacles in a wide, shallow dish and sprinkle with the herb leaves, coriander seeds, chile, garlic, lemon rind, and the juice of 1 lemon. Drizzle over 2–3 tbsp (30–45ml) olive oil and toss the squid to coat all over with the marinade. Cover with plastic wrap and let marinate in the refrigerator for 20 to 30 minutes.

Heat the barbecue or a stovetop grill pan. Transfer the squid to a plate, ready to cook, scraping off and reserving the excess marinade.

Pat the roasted peppers with paper towels to absorb excess oil, then slice into strips. Heat the reserved marinade from the squid in a sauté pan and add the peppers, beans, remaining lemon juice, and some seasoning. Sauté for 3 to 5 minutes to heat through. Set aside.

Place the squid on the barbecue or grill pan, laying the scored pieces flat. Cook until the squid turns opaque, about 1 minute on each side for the scored pieces, a little longer for the tentacles. Remove to a plate. When cool enough to handle, slice the squid body into strips and cut the tentacles in half.

Stir the sliced squid and chopped parsley through the warm peppers and beans. Serve immediately.

Grilled sardines with chermoula

a healthy boost of omega-3 fatty acids

Serves 4

8 very fresh sardines, cleaned

sea salt and black pepper

little olive oil, to drizzle

Chermoula:

2 tsp (10ml) cumin seeds

2 tsp (10ml) coriander seeds

2 garlic cloves, peeled and roughly chopped

1 tsp (5ml) sweet paprika

finely grated rind and juice of 1 small lemon

4–5 tbsp (60–75ml) extra-virgin olive oil

small handful of cilantro, chopped

To make the chermoula, toast the cumin and coriander seeds in a pan over low heat until fragrant. Tip into a mortar and add a pinch each of salt and pepper. Grind to a fine powder, then add the garlic and grind the mixture to a paste. Stir in the rest of the ingredients.

Score the sardines lightly on both sides at ½-inch (1cm) intervals and place in a shallow dish. Pour half of the chermoula mixture over the fish and rub the marinade into the scored skin. Cover with plastic wrap and let marinate in the refrigerator for at least 1 hour, or up to 4 hours.

Heat the barbecue or the broiler to high. Season the sardines with a little salt and pepper and oil lightly. Place them in a sandwich-style wire barbecue rack, or on a wide, oiled baking sheet if broiling. Barbecue for 3 minutes each side, or broil for 4 to 5 minutes each side, basting with the pan juices as you turn them halfway.

Transfer the sardines to a warm platter, spoon over the remaining chermoula, and serve with saffron rice pilaf or zesty couscous.

114

Spelt focaccia with rosemary and garlic

Serves 6

½oz (15g) fresh yeast or ¼oz (7g) active dry yeast

1 cup (250ml) lukewarm water

1½ cups (200g) spelt flour

1½ cups (200g) Italian "00" grade flour, plus extra to dust

1 tsp (5ml) fine sea salt, plus extra to sprinkle (optional)

2 tbsp (30ml) chopped rosemary leaves, plus extra whole leaves for sprinkling

6–7 garlic cloves, 2 peeled and finely crushed, the rest in their skins

about ¼ cup (50ml) extra-virgin olive oil, plus extra to drizzle

If using fresh yeast, put 2–3 tbsp (30–45ml) of the lukewarm water in a small bowl and crumble in the yeast. Stir to dissolve and leave for 10 to 15 minutes to foam.

Sift the flours and salt together into a large bowl, tipping in the bran left in the strainer. If using active dry yeast, add it at this stage. Stir in the chopped rosemary.

Make a well in the center. Add the crushed garlic, then pour in the yeast liquid (if using fresh yeast), olive oil, and most of the remaining water. Stir with a wooden spoon until the mixture comes together. Add the rest of the water as necessary, a little at a time, to form a soft but not sticky dough.

Press the dough together then tip it onto a lightly floured counter. Knead for about 5 minutes to form a smooth, elastic dough. Place in a lightly oiled large mixing bowl, cover with a clean dish towel, and let rise in a warm spot for about 2 hours until the dough has doubled in size.

Heat the oven to 400°F (200°C). Turn the dough onto a lightly floured counter and knead lightly. Place on a well-oiled baking sheet and gently flatten with the palms of your hands. Pull and shape it toward the edges of the baking sheet to form a ½-inch (1cm) thick rectangle. Press with your fingertips to create indentations in the dough.

Stud the dough randomly with rosemary leaves and whole garlic cloves and drizzle over a little olive oil. If you wish, sprinkle over a little sea salt. Bake for 15 to 20 minutes until golden brown. Let cool slightly. Slice and serve warm.

lightly spiced and enhanced with a zingy salsa

Tandoori poussins
with mango relish

Serves 4

4 poussins, about 14oz–1lb
(400–500g) each

Tandoori marinade:

1 tsp (5ml) ground turmeric

2 tsp (10ml) garam masala

1 tsp (5ml) ground coriander

1 tsp (5ml) ground cumin

1 large garlic clove, peeled and finely crushed

1¼-inch (3cm) piece of gingerroot, peeled and finely grated

juice of ½ lemon

generous ⅓ cup (100ml) plain yogurt

small handful of cilantro stalks, minced

sea salt and black pepper

Mango relish:

1 firm but ripe mango

1 large red onion, peeled and minced

1 red chile, seeded and minced

juice of ½ lime

To spatchcock the poussins hold one, breast side down, on a cutting board. Using a pair of kitchen scissors, snip along both sides of the backbone to remove it. Turn the poussin over and press firmly down the middle with the palm of your hand to flatten it. Cut off the wing tip and trim off the excess skin and fat. Repeat with the remaining birds.

For the marinade, mix all the ingredients together in a large shallow bowl. Add the poussins and turn them over so that each bird is well coated. Cover with plastic wrap and let marinate in the refrigerator for several hours, or overnight.

Heat the oven to 325°F (170°C). Transfer the poussins to a large baking sheet, pour on the marinade from the bowl, and sprinkle with some salt and pepper. Cover with foil and bake for 30 to 40 minutes until just cooked through. To test, prick the thickest part of each poussin with a skewer and press gently— the juices should run clear. Take off the foil and cool.

Make the mango relish in the meantime. Peel the mango and chop the flesh, discarding the seed. Place in a bowl with the onion, chile, and lime juice. Toss to mix and season with salt and pepper to taste. Cover with plastic wrap and chill for 20 minutes.

Heat the barbecue or a stovetop grill pan until hot. Cook the poussins for 8 to 10 minutes, turning them over halfway, until nicely charred on both sides. Rest for a few minutes before serving, with the mango relish on the side.

Beef burgers with beet relish and cucumber raita

Serves 4

1⅓lb (600g) good quality ground beef

1 tsp (5ml) smoked paprika

pinch of cayenne pepper

sea salt and black pepper

olive oil, to cook and drizzle

8oz (250g) cherry tomatoes on the vine

splash of balsamic vinegar

4 iceberg lettuce leaves, trimmed to neaten (optional)

handful of wild arugula leaves (optional)

Beet relish:

8oz (250g) cooked beet in natural juices, drained

3 tbsp capers, rinsed and drained

handful of Italian parsley, roughly chopped

2 tbsp (30ml) balsamic vinegar

3 tbsp (45ml) olive oil

Cucumber raita:

1 large cucumber

handful of mint leaves, chopped

3–4 tbsp (45–60ml) plain yogurt

squeeze of lemon juice, to taste

Put the ground beef into a large bowl and add the paprika, cayenne, ½ tsp (2ml) salt (or less to taste) and ½ tsp (2ml) pepper. Mix well with your hands, then shape into 4 neat patties. Place on a plate or tray, cover with plastic wrap, and chill for at least 30 minutes to set the shape.

Make the beet relish in the meantime. Roughly chop the beet and place in a food processor along with the capers, parsley, balsamic vinegar, and olive oil. Pulse until the mixture is roughly chopped—you don't want to purée the beet. Season to taste and transfer to a bowl.

For the cucumber raita, peel the cucumber and quarter lengthwise. Scrape out the seeds with a spoon and discard. Roughly chop the flesh and place in a bowl. Add the chopped mint and toss with enough yogurt to bind. Add the lemon juice and season with salt and pepper to taste.

Heat the barbecue or heat a little olive oil in a nonstick skillet. Brush the burgers with olive oil and cook on the barbecue, or pan-fry allowing 3½ to 4 minutes on each side for medium burgers. Remove to a warm plate and let rest for a few minutes. Add the tomatoes to the barbecue or skillet and drizzle with a little olive oil and balsamic vinegar. Cook for 1 to 2 minutes until the tomatoes are soft but still retain their shape.

Serve the burgers with the tomatoes, beet relish, and cucumber raita. For a neat presentation, spoon the raita into lettuce cups and garnish with a handful of arugula.

Lamb kabobs with peppers and tomatoes

1lb (500g) lean lamb leg steaks

1 large sweet red pepper

1 large sweet yellow pepper

8 crimini mushrooms

8 cherry tomatoes, peeled if preferred

olive oil, to drizzle

Herb paste:

finely grated rind and juice of 1 lemon

2 garlic cloves, peeled and minced

½ tsp (2ml) dried oregano

½ tsp (2ml) dried mint

½ tsp (2ml) dried thyme

¼ tsp (1ml) dried ground rosemary

½ tsp (2ml) dried tarragon

1 tbsp (15ml) olive oil

sea salt and black pepper

Cut the lamb steaks into 1-inch (2.5cm) cubes and place in a bowl. Stir together all the ingredients for the herb paste and pour over the lamb. Toss well to coat the pieces evenly. Cover the bowl with plastic wrap and let marinate in the refrigerator for several hours, or overnight. Soak 6–8 bamboo skewers in cold water for at least 20 minutes.

Halve the peppers, remove the core and seeds, then cut into 1-inch (2.5cm) pieces. Thread the peppers, lamb, mushrooms, and cherry tomatoes alternately onto the soaked bamboo skewers.

Heat the barbecue or place a stovetop grill pan over high heat. Drizzle a little olive oil over the skewers and sprinkle with some salt and pepper. Barbecue or grill the skewers for 2½ to 3 minutes on each side. Let rest for a minute or two, then serve with side salads of your choice.

succulent, lean lamb marinated in a herb paste

5 ways with
tomatoes

Mass-produced tomatoes picked before they've had a chance to ripen are usually tasteless. Vine-ripened tomatoes at their peak are altogether different. Recently, I visited an amazing organic farm in Wales. There must have been more than 20 different varieties of tomatoes slowly ripening on the vines. I was wide-eyed like a child in a candy store, taking in the varied colors and shapes of this versatile fruit.

Tomatoes are incredibly good for you. They are a useful source of nutrients, including vitamin C and Beta carotene, which the body converts to vitamin A. Probably their greatest asset, though, is the powerful antioxidant lycopene, which helps to protect the body from disease. Vine-ripened tomatoes are staples in our home kitchen—finding their way into salads, sauces, and all manner of cooked dishes.

1

Mixed tomato salad Use 2lb (1kg) mixed vine-ripened tomatoes (including some cherry tomatoes). Halve or quarter the larger ones and place in a large bowl with the cherry tomatoes. Add 2 sliced green onions and a handful of torn basil leaves. Dress with a squeeze of lemon juice, a drizzle of olive oil, and salt and pepper to taste. Serve at room temperarture to appreciate the flavors to the full. **Serves 4–6**

2

Pasta with quick tomato sauce Boil 10oz (300g) dried penne pasta in a pot of salted water until al dente. Meanwhile, in a blender, whiz 6 ripe plum tomatoes, 2 chopped garlic cloves, a chopped piece of ginger, 2 tbsp (30ml) cider vinegar or lemon juice, 1 tbsp (15ml) brown sugar, 1 tbsp (15ml) tomato paste, and the stalks from a handful of cilantro until smooth. Tip the mixture into a pan, season, and simmer for 5 minutes. Drain the pasta, toss with a little olive oil, and divide between warm bowls. Spoon over the tomato sauce and sprinkle with cilantro leaves. **Serves 4**

3 **Chunky gazpacho** Mince 6 ripe plum tomatoes, 1 small red onion, 1 sweet red pepper, and ½ cucumber (peeled and seeded). Place in a large bowl, add a crushed garlic clove, and sprinkle over the juice of ½–1 lemon, to taste. Season with salt and pepper and stir well. Pour over 1¼ cups (300ml) cold chicken or vegetable stock and 1¼ cups (300ml) tomato juice to cover, then stir in a dash each of Tabasco and Worcestershire sauce and some chopped basil and tarragon. Cover with plastic wrap and chill for at least 4 hours to let the flavors develop. Serve in chilled bowls. **Serves 4**

4 **Stuffed beefsteak tomatoes** Heat oven to 400°F (200°C). Put ½ cup (100g) couscous in a heatproof bowl with a pinch each of saffron strands, salt, and pepper. Pour on ½ cup (125ml) boiling hot chicken stock or water, cover, and leave for 5 minutes. Cut off the top third of each of 4 large beefsteak tomatoes; set aside.

Scoop the seeds into a bowl. Scoop out the flesh to hollow out the tomatoes, mince, and add to the seeds with a chopped handful each of cilantro and mint, 3 sliced green onions, the juice of ½–1 lemon, 4 tbsp (60ml) toasted pine nuts, scant ¼ cup (30g) golden raisins, and 2–3 tbsp (30–45ml) olive oil. Mix well and season to taste. Fluff up the couscous with a fork and stir in the tomato seed mixture. Spoon into the tomato shells and top with the lids. Place on a lightly oiled baking sheet and bake for 15 to 20 minutes until soft. **Serves 4**

5 **Homemade ketchup** Peel and chop 1lb (500g) ripe plum tomatoes. Heat 1 tbsp (15ml) olive oil in a pan and sweat 1 chopped sweet onion with 2 chopped garlic cloves over medium-low heat for 4 to 6 minutes until softened. Lightly crush ½ tsp (2ml) each fennel and coriander seeds and add to the vegetables with some seasoning. Cook, stirring, for ½ minute, then add the chopped tomatoes, 1¼ cups (300ml) tomato juice or water, ¼ cup (50g) light brown sugar, 1 tbsp (15ml) red wine vinegar, and a few basil sprigs. Simmer gently for 25 to 30 minutes or until the mixture is thick and the tomatoes are soft and pulpy. Adjust the seasoning and sweetness, adding a little more sugar or vinegar if needed. Whiz in a food processor or blender to a purée, then pass through a fine strainer into a bowl and cool. **Makes 1¼ cups (300ml)**

Four cabbage coleslaw

low in calories and cholesterol, high in fiber

Serves 4

¼ Chinese cabbage

¼ savoy cabbage

¼ white cabbage

¼ red cabbage

handful of chives, finely snipped

Dressing:

3 tbsp (45ml) extra-virgin olive oil

1 tbsp (15ml) sesame oil

2 tbsp (30ml) balsamic vinegar

2 tbsp (30ml) whole grain mustard

sea salt and black pepper

Cut out the core from each cabbage, then finely shred the leaves with a sharp knife. Place in a large bowl and toss well to mix.

For the dressing, whisk all the ingredients together in a bowl, seasoning with salt and pepper to taste. Pour over the shredded cabbage and toss to mix. Let marinate for at least 20 minutes before serving.

Sprinkle the chives over the coleslaw and toss to mix just before serving.

Fennel, pea, and fava bean salad

Serves 4

2 medium fennel bulbs

4 large eggs, at room temperature

1²/₃ cups (250g) shelled fava beans

2½ cups (250g) shelled peas, thawed if frozen

olive oil, to drizzle

8 prosciutto slices

Dressing:

1 small garlic clove, peeled and finely crushed

1 tsp (5ml) superfine sugar, or to taste

1 tbsp (15ml) lemon juice

1 tbsp (15ml) whole grain mustard

3 tbsp (45ml) extra-virgin olive oil

handful of dill, roughly chopped

sea salt and black pepper

Trim the fennel, cutting off the base and removing the coarse outer layer of leaves. Cut each bulb in half lengthwise, then slice as thinly as possible, using a mandolin or a sharp knife. Place in a large bowl of iced water and let soak for about 10 to 15 minutes to crisp up.

Meanwhile, add the eggs to a pan of simmering water and simmer for 9 minutes (the yolks should be set but still quite soft). Immediately drain, then refresh in a pan of cold water.

Bring another pan of water to a boil. Add the fava beans and blanch for 1 minute, then add the peas and return to a boil. Blanch for another 3 minutes until the peas and fava beans are tender. Drain and refresh in a bowl of iced water.

For the dressing, whisk all the ingredients together in a bowl, seasoning with salt and pepper to taste.

Add the fava beans and peas to the fennel. Pour over the dressing and toss well. Shell the eggs, then cut into quarters lengthwise.

When ready to serve, heat a tiny drizzle of olive oil in a nonstick pan and pan-fry the prosciutto until golden and crisp, turning once. Divide the salad and eggs between serving plates. Break the crispy prosciutto into smaller pieces and sprinkle over the salads. Sprinkle with pepper and serve.

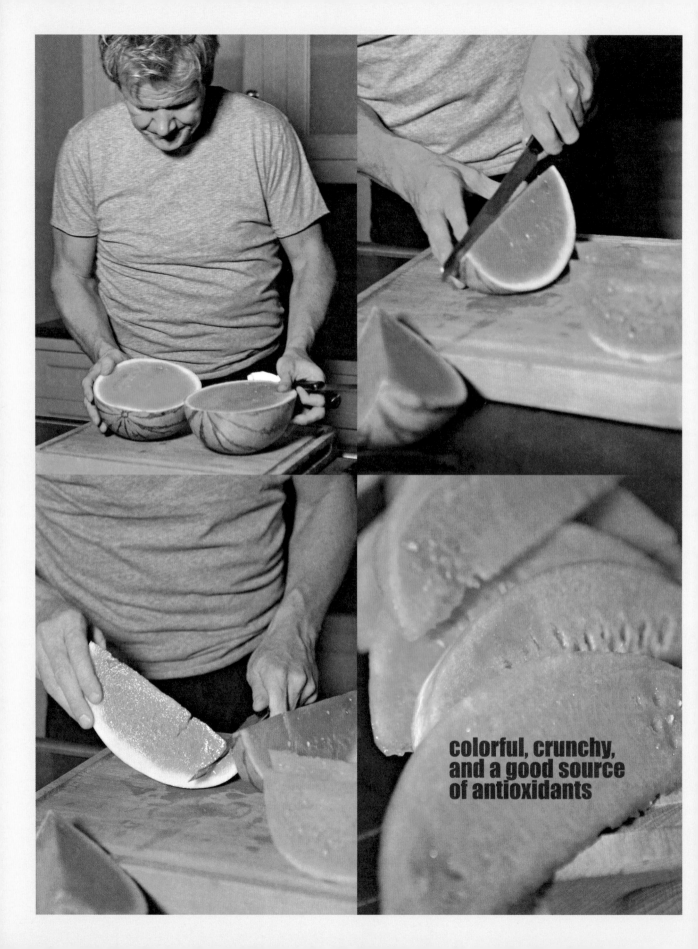

colorful, crunchy, and a good source of antioxidants

Shrimp, feta, and watermelon salad

Serves 4

7oz (200g) raw shrimp, peeled and deveined

2 tbsp (30ml) olive oil

pinch of cayenne pepper

sea salt and black pepper

3lb (1.5kg) ripe seedless watermelon

1³⁄₄oz (50g) wild arugula leaves, washed

4oz (120g) feta cheese

1 tbsp (15ml) toasted mixed seeds, such as pumpkin and sunflower seeds

Dressing:

2 tbsp (30ml) lime juice

½ tsp (2ml) superfine sugar

4 tbsp (60ml) extra-virgin olive oil

Marinate the shrimp by tossing them together with 1 tbsp (15ml) olive oil, a pinch of cayenne, and some salt and pepper in a bowl. Cover with plastic wrap and let marinate in the refrigerator for 10 to 15 minutes.

Cut the watermelon into wedges, then cut off the skin and slice the flesh thinly. Layer the watermelon slices on a large serving platter, interleaving them with arugula leaves. Crumble over the feta and grind over some black pepper.

Place a large skillet, preferably a nonstick one, over medium heat and add 1 tbsp (15ml) olive oil. Tip in the shrimp and pan-fry for about 2 minutes until they turn opaque, flipping them over after a minute or so. Transfer to a plate and let cool slightly while you make the dressing.

Whisk the dressing ingredients together and season to taste. Add the shrimp to the platter and sprinkle over the seeds, if using. Drizzle with the dressing and serve.

Beet, carrot, and chicory salad with pomegranate dressing

loaded with vitamins, minerals, and antioxidants

Serves 4

3 heads of chicory

2 medium carrots

8oz (250g) cooked beet in natural juices

handful of toasted hazelnuts, lightly crushed (optional)

Dressing:

1 pomegranate

1 orange

2 tbsp (30ml) balsamic vinegar

3–4 tbsp (45–60ml) extra-virgin olive oil

sea salt and black pepper

Trim the chicory, cutting off the base, then shred the leaves into thin sticks. Peel the carrots and cut them into ribbons, using a swivel vegetable peeler. Mix the chicory and carrot ribbons together in a salad bowl. Roughly cut the beet into quarters and add to the bowl.

For the dressing, halve the pomegranate and scoop out the seeds and juice into a bowl, picking out and discarding any membrane. Similarly, cut the orange in half and squeeze the juice into the bowl. Add the balsamic vinegar, olive oil, and seasoning to taste. Blitz the mixture using a hand-held stick blender (or free-standing blender) until the pomegranate seeds are finely crushed. Pass the mixture through a fine strainer, pressing down on the pulp with the back of a spoon.

Spoon the dressing over the salad (any extra will keep in the refrigerator for a few days). Sprinkle a handful of toasted hazelnuts over the salad to serve if you like.

Baked stuffed figs
with goat cheese and pine nuts

a fantastic way to finish a barbecue

Serves 4

8 ripe figs

3½oz (100g) soft goat cheese

handful of chives, finely snipped

good quality balsamic vinegar, to drizzle

few thyme sprigs, leaves stripped

2 tbsp (30ml) toasted pine nuts

Trim off the tip from each fig, then cut a cross through the top, cutting about halfway down. Squeeze the base of the figs to open out the top quarters like a flower.

Stuff the figs with the goat cheese, sprinkle with snipped chives, and drizzle with balsamic vinegar. Sprinkle over the thyme leaves and pine nuts.

Stand the figs on a large piece of foil. Bring up the sides and fold together to seal the package. You can either bake the figs in a hot oven, preheated to 400°F (200°C), or on a barbecue. They should take about 10 to 12 minutes. Unwrap the package and serve immediately, as an appetizer, an accompaniment, or to round off a meal.

omega-3 boost

Oily fish are an excellent source of omega-3 fatty acids, which offer several health benefits. Studies have indicated a lower incidence of cardiovascular disease among those who consume oily fish regularly. It is thought that these essential fatty acids improve the flow of blood through smaller blood vessels, helping to reduce the chances of blood clots, and ultimately, the risk of strokes and heart attacks. Omega-3's also have anti-inflammatory properties. There is some evidence to suggest that they may improve brainpower and concentration, too. Certainly these fatty acids are important for healthy brain and nerve development, so they are particularly valuable for children and pregnant moms.

Other sources of omega-3 fatty acids include flaxseed, walnuts, and walnut oil. However, oily fish is deemed to be the richest source.

Eating oily fish more often—ideally once or twice a week—is the best way to obtain your omega-3's. Don't get yourself into a rut, though. Try a different type of fish each time and vary the way you cook and serve them. Of course they are delicious simply broiled or pan-fried with the minimum of oil and served with a tomato or leafy salad to cut the richness, but you can also turn these fish into tasty pâtés (see page 170). And don't forget to opt for the sustainable varieties, such as trout, bream, sardines, mackerel, and herrings.

Healthy suppers

Fish cakes with anchovy dressing

Serves 4

14oz (400g) waxy potatoes

2 tbsp (30ml) olive oil

finely grated rind of 1 large lemon

2–3 tbsp (30–45ml) lemon juice

sea salt and black pepper

few thyme sprigs

½ lemon, sliced

10oz (300g) salmon fillet

10oz (300g) smoked haddock fillet

handful of Italian parsley, chopped

handful of chervil, chopped

3 tbsp (45ml) all-purpose flour

2 medium eggs, lightly beaten

1 cup (50g) Japanese panko bread crumbs

2 tbsp (30ml) olive oil

Anchovy dressing:

2 tbsp (30ml) capers

2 shallots, peeled and minced

bunch of Italian parsley, leaves only, chopped

4 marinated anchovies, chopped

4 tbsp (60ml) extra-virgin olive oil

Peel the potatoes, cut into even-size pieces, and drop into a pan of well salted water. Bring to a boil and cook for 10 to 15 minutes until tender when pierced with a knife. Drain well. While still hot, mash the potatoes using a potato ricer back into the pan. Mix in the olive oil, lemon rind, lemon juice, and seasoning to taste. Let cool.

Meanwhile, add the thyme, lemon slices, and salmon to a wide pan of slowly simmering salted water and poach for a minute. Slide in the smoked haddock and gently poach for another 4 to 5 minutes until both fish are almost cooked through. Transfer to a plate, using a spatula. When cool enough to handle, break the fish into large flakes, discarding the skin and pin-bones.

Mix the fish and chopped herbs into the mashed potatoes, using your hands. Taste and adjust the seasoning. Divide the mixture into four and shape into neat patties. Season the flour with salt and pepper. Coat the fish cakes in seasoned flour, then dip into the egg and finally into the bread crumbs, turning to coat evenly all over. Reshape them as necessary and place on a tray or plate. Chill for 2 hours to set the shape.

To cook, heat the oven to 350°F (180°C). Heat a thin layer of olive oil in a wide ovenproof skillet. Pan-fry the fish cakes for 2 to 3 minutes until golden, then flip over and cook the other side for 1 to 2 minutes. Finish cooking in the oven for 5 to 7 minutes.

Make the dressing in the meantime, by gently warming all the ingredients together in a pan for 3 to 4 minutes. Spread a generous spoonful of dressing on each warm plate and rest a fish cake in the center. Serve immediately, with peas or beans.

Glazed Cod with sweet 'n' sour shallots

Serves 4

4 skinless cod fillets, about 6oz (170g) each

a little olive oil, for oiling

4 tbsp (60ml) light soy sauce

2 tbsp (30ml) dark soy sauce

1/3 cup (100ml) white wine vinegar

1/4 cup (50g) soft brown sugar

1 tsp (5ml) coriander seeds, lightly crushed

1 tsp (5ml) black peppercorns, crushed

1 1/4-inch (3cm) piece of gingerroot, peeled and finely grated

14oz (400g) small shallots, peeled

5 tbsp (75ml) dry white wine

2/3 cup (150ml) fish stock (see page 248)

small handful of chives, snipped

Lay the fish fillets in an oiled large baking dish and set aside. Put the soy sauces, wine vinegar, and sugar in a pan and stir over low heat to dissolve the sugar. Increase the heat and tip in the coriander seeds, peppercorns, and ginger. Boil for 8 to 10 minutes until the liquid has reduced by half. Cool completely.

Heat the oven to 350°F (180°C). Blanch the shallots in a pan of boiling water for 10 minutes until tender, then drain.

Pour the soy mixture over the cod fillets and cook in the oven for 5 minutes until the sauce begins to caramelize. Sprinkle the blanched shallots around the fish and pour on the white wine and fish stock. Return to the oven and bake for 6 to 8 minutes until the fish is just cooked through.

Transfer the fish to a warm plate, using a spatula. Cover with foil and set aside to rest in a warm place for 5 to 10 minutes. Meanwhile, tip the onions and liquor into a pan and boil for 10 minutes until reduced to a sticky sauce.

Place the fish on warm plates and spoon over the shallots and sauce. Garnish with snipped chives and serve with steamed rice and stir-fried bok choy, if you wish.

Note You can use any firm white fish instead.

142

rich in protein, low in fat

Spiced monkfish
with crushed potatoes, peppers, and olives

Serves 4

4 monkfish tail fillets, skinned, about 6oz (170g) each

1 tsp (5ml) five-spice powder

1 tsp (5ml) sweet paprika

1 tsp (5ml) salt

2 tbsp (30ml) olive oil

handful of Italian parsley, chopped

lemon wedges, to serve

Crushed potatoes:

1½lb (750g) new potatoes, scraped clean

sea salt and black pepper

2 tbsp (30ml) extra-virgin olive oil

squeeze of lemon juice

7oz (200g) drained roasted peppers in oil (from a jar), chopped

½ cup (75g) pitted black olives, chopped

handful of basil leaves, shredded

Heat the oven to 400°F (200°C). Next, to cook the potatoes, add them to a pan of well salted boiling water and cook for about 10 to 15 minutes until tender.

Lay the monkfish on a board and remove any grayish membrane. Mix the five-spice powder, paprika, and salt together on a plate. Roll the monkfish fillets in the spice mixture to coat evenly all over. Place a roasting pan in the oven to heat up.

Heat the olive oil in a heavy skillet and sear the monkfish fillets, in batches if necessary, for 1½ to 2 minutes on each side until golden brown all over. Transfer the monkfish fillets to the hot roasting pan and bake for 8 to 10 minutes until the fish is just cooked through. When ready, remove from the oven, cover with foil, and let rest for 5 minutes.

Drain the potatoes as soon as they are done and return to the pan. Lightly crush them with the back of a fork or a potato masher and mix in the extra-virgin olive oil, lemon juice, and some seasoning. Stir in the chopped peppers, olives, and basil. Taste and adjust the seasoning.

Cut the monkfish into thick slices. Spoon the crushed potatoes onto warm serving plates and arrange the monkfish on top. Sprinkle with the chopped parsley and serve at once, with lemon wedges and spinach or broccoli.

Seared yellowfin tuna with black beans

flavorful protein-packed meal

Serves 4

4 yellowfin tuna steaks, about 7oz (200g) each and ¾ inch (2cm) thick

sea salt and black pepper

1 tsp (5ml) coriander seeds, lightly crushed

4 tsp–2 tbsp (20–30ml) olive oil

Black beans:

1¼ cups (200g) black beans, soaked overnight

few thyme sprigs

1 bay leaf

1 onion, peeled and halved

1 carrot, peeled and cut into 3 chunks

3–4 tbsp (45–60ml) olive oil

2 red onions, peeled and minced

1 garlic clove, peeled and minced

6 green onions, trimmed and finely sliced

handful of cilantro leaves, chopped

juice of ½ lemon juice, or to taste

Cook the beans first. Drain, then tip into a large pan and add the thyme, bay leaf, onion, and carrot. Pour in enough water to cover by 1½ inches (4cm). Bring to a simmer and cook for 40 to 50 minutes until the beans are soft. Remove the herbs, carrot, and onion and discard. Drain the beans and let cool.

Heat a skillet and add 3 tbsp (45ml) olive oil. Tip in the red onions and garlic and cook, stirring frequently, for 4 to 6 minutes until they begin to soften but not brown. Stir in the black beans and cook for a few minutes to warm through. Use a fork to roughly mash the beans in the pan or gently pound with the end of a rolling pin—leaving some whole for a varied texture. If the mixture looks dry, add another 1 tbsp (15ml) olive oil and a splash of water, then mix through the green onions, cilantro, and lemon juice. Season with salt and pepper to taste. Keep warm while you cook the tuna.

Season the tuna with salt and pepper and coat one side of the steaks with the crushed coriander seeds. Heat a skillet, add the olive oil, and pan-fry the steaks for 2 minutes on each side. Transfer to a warm plate, cover with foil, and let rest for a few minutes.

Divide the beans between warm serving plates and lay the tuna steaks on top. Serve at once.

Herby crayfish
and shrimp pilaf

plenty of essential minerals and B vitamins

Serves 4

2–3 tbsp (30–45ml) olive oil

3 small or 2 large red onions, peeled and thinly sliced

1¼ cups (250g) basmati rice

finely pared rind of 2 lemons

few thyme sprigs

2 garlic cloves (unpeeled), lightly smashed

sea salt and black pepper

generous 2 cups (550ml) hot fish stock (see page 248)

1½lb (750g) live crayfish, washed

8oz (250g) large raw shrimp

handful of chives, finely snipped

handful of basil leaves, finely sliced

handful of chervil leaves, roughly chopped

Heat the oven to 375°F (190°C). Cut a waxed paper circle slightly larger than a heavy ovenproof pan or a cast-iron casserole. Snip a small hole in the middle of the paper to act as a steam vent.

Heat the pan with the olive oil, then sauté the onions for 4 to 6 minutes until they begin to soften. Stir in the rice, lemon rind, thyme, garlic, and some seasoning. Stir well to toast the rice for a couple of minutes. Pour in the hot fish stock and bring to a boil. Add the crayfish to the pan and quickly cover with the waxed paper. Transfer the pan to the oven.

After 15 minutes, take the pan out of the oven, lift the waxed paper, and sprinkle over the shrimp. Re-cover with the waxed paper and return to the oven for 10 minutes until the rice is tender and the shrimp are just cooked through and opaque. Remove from the oven and let stand for about 5 minutes before lifting off the paper.

Fork through the rice to distribute the shellfish evenly. Check the seasoning and stir in the chopped herbs. Serve at once.

148

Steamed shrimp
with black bean sauce

Serves 4

1lb (500g) large raw shrimp

5–6 Chinese cabbage leaves

sea salt

2 green onions, trimmed

Sauce:

4 tsp (20ml) sunflower oil

1 large garlic clove, peeled and finely crushed

1¼-inch (3cm) piece of gingerroot, peeled and finely crushed

pinch of hot red pepper flakes

4 tsp–2 tbsp (20–30ml) fermented black beans (available from Asian food stores)

5 tbsp (75ml) chicken stock (see page 249)

2 tbsp (30ml) light soy sauce

2 tbsp (30ml) rice wine

1 tbsp (15ml) mirin

2 tsp (10ml) superfine sugar, or to taste

1 tsp (5ml) cornstarch, mixed with 1 tbsp (15ml) water

First, make the sauce. Heat the oil in a pan and add the garlic, ginger, pepper flakes, and black beans. Stir-fry for a couple of minutes, then pour in the stock, soy sauce, rice wine, and mirin. Bring to a simmer, then stir in the sugar and cornstarch mixture. Simmer for a few minutes, stirring frequently, until the sauce has thickened. Pour into a wide bowl and let cool.

Peel the shrimp and devein them, by cutting a slit along the back and removing the dark thread. Bring a large pan of water (that will hold a large steamer basket) to a boil. If you don't have a steamer, overturn a heatproof bowl in a large pan or wok (with lid) and pour in enough hot water to come halfway up the sides of the bowl. Bring to a simmer.

Blanch the cabbage leaves in boiling salted water for 2 to 3 minutes. Drain well and use to line a large, shallow heatproof bowl (that will fit in the steamer), trimming the edges of the leaves as necessary.

Arrange the shrimp on the cabbage and spoon the sauce over them. Place in the steamer and cook for 8 to 9 minutes until the shrimp are just firm and opaque. Meanwhile, finely slice the green onions on the diagonal.

Sprinkle the green onions over the shrimp and serve with steamed rice and stir-fried vegetables.

Thai-style beef stir-fry

Serves 4

14oz (400g) beef filet, trimmed and cut into thin strips

1 garlic clove, peeled and chopped

¾-inch (2cm) piece of gingerroot, peeled and chopped

½ red chile, trimmed and roughly sliced

5oz (150g) crimini mushrooms, trimmed and thinly sliced

1 carrot, peeled and thinly sliced on the diagonal

1 sweet red pepper, cored, seeded, and sliced into thin strips

5oz (150g) snow peas

2 green onions, trimmed and sliced on the diagonal

sea salt and black pepper

3 tbsp (45ml) sunflower oil

handful of Thai sweet basil (or cilantro) leaves, to garnish

Sauce:

2 tbsp (30ml) light soy sauce

3 tbsp (45ml) oyster sauce

1 tbsp (15ml) rice vinegar

1 tsp (5ml) superfine sugar

1 tsp (5ml) cornstarch

3–4 tbsp (45–60ml) water

Have the beef and all the aromatic ingredients and vegetables chopped and ready before you begin to cook.

For the sauce, mix all the ingredients together in a small bowl and set aside. Lightly season the beef strips with salt and pepper.

Heat a wok or a large skillet until hot then add a little oil, swirling the wok to coat the surface evenly. Add half the beef strips and stir-fry for about a minute until just brown on the surface, but still medium rare in the middle. Remove to a plate and repeat with the remaining beef. Set the beef aside.

Add a little more oil to the wok along with the garlic, ginger, and chile. Stir-fry the mixture for about a minute until lightly golden and fragrant. Toss in the mushrooms and stir-fry for a minute. Add the carrot and a splash of water. (This will create steam, to help cook the vegetables evenly.) After a minute, toss in the red pepper and snow peas. Stir-fry for another 2 minutes or until the vegetables are just tender.

Give the sauce a stir and pour over the vegetables, then return the beef to the wok. Toss over the heat for another minute until the sauce has thickened. Turn off the heat and stir in the green onions.

Spoon the stir-fry onto warm serving plates and sprinkle over the basil leaves. Serve at once, with steamed jasmine rice.

Vietnamese beef and noodle soup

Serves 4

1lb (500g) beef filet

1-inch (2.5cm) piece of gingerroot, peeled and finely grated

1 large garlic clove, peeled and finely crushed

sea salt and black pepper

1 tbsp (15ml) sesame oil, plus extra to toss

7oz (200g) dried thin rice noodles

5oz (150g) bean sprouts

2–3 green onions, trimmed and thinly sliced on the diagonal

small bunch of cilantro, leaves only

small bunch of mint or Thai sweet basil, leaves only

Broth:

6 cups (1.5 liters) beef stock (see page 249)

1½-inch (4cm) piece of gingerroot, peeled and thinly sliced

4 star anise

3 cloves

2 cinnamon sticks

1 cardamom pod, lightly crushed

2 tsp (10ml) superfine sugar, or to taste

3 tbsp (45ml) fish sauce

To serve:

lime wedges

hoisin sauce

Vietnamese chili sauce

Trim the beef of any sinew, then slice as thinly as possible. Place in a bowl and add the grated ginger, garlic, some pepper, and the sesame oil. Toss to mix, cover, and let marinate in the refrigerator for 30 to 40 minutes.

For the broth, pour the beef stock into a large pan and add the rest of the ingredients with a little salt and pepper. Bring to a boil, lower the heat, and simmer for about 30 minutes. Strain the broth into a clean pan, discarding the ginger and spices. Taste and adjust the seasoning.

Add the rice noodles to a large pan of boiling salted water and cook according to the package directions until tender, but still retaining a bite. Drain in a colander and immediately toss the noodles with a little sesame oil to prevent them from sticking.

Bring the broth to a boil and tip in the beef and bean sprouts. Simmer for just 30 seconds, then remove from the heat.

Divide the noodles among warm bowls and ladle the hot broth over them, dividing the beef and bean sprouts equally. Sprinkle over the green onions, cilantro, and mint. Serve immediately, with lime wedges and little individual dishes of hoisin and Vietnamese chili sauces for dipping.

Spiced pork chops
with sweet potatoes

Serves 4

4 pork loin chops with bone, about 10oz (300g) each

½–1 tsp (2–5ml) mild chili powder, to taste

1 tsp (5ml) sweet paprika

sea salt and black pepper

2 tbsp (30ml) olive oil

few thyme sprigs

4 garlic cloves (unpeeled), lightly smashed

5–6 star anise, lightly smashed

1 tsp (5ml) coriander seeds, lightly crushed

3 large sweet potatoes, about ⅔lb (350g)

1 red chile, trimmed, seeded, and minced

bunch of cilantro, chopped

Cut off the rind and excess fat around the pork chops. Mix the chili powder, paprika, and some salt and pepper with the olive oil in a wide baking dish. Add the thyme, garlic, star anise, and coriander seeds. Add the pork chops and turn to coat. Cover and let marinate for at least 30 minutes, or in the refrigerator overnight.

Heat the oven to 350°F (180°C). Bake the pork chops, uncovered, for about 15 minutes until the meat is just firm when lightly pressed.

Meanwhile, bring a pan of salted water to a boil. Peel the sweet potatoes and cut into ⅝-inch (1.5cm) slices. Add to the pan and cook for 7 to 8 minutes until almost tender when pierced with a skewer. (They should be slightly undercooked at this stage.) Drain and refresh under cold running water. Dice the potatoes; set aside.

When cooked, transfer the chops to a warm plate, cover with foil, and rest in a warm place for 10 minutes. Squeeze out the soft garlic from the skins and return to the baking dish. Add the chile, tip in the sweet potatoes, and toss to mix. Season lightly and bake for 10 minutes, stirring once or twice, until the potatoes are tender.

Stir the coriander through the sweet potatoes and spoon onto warm plates. Add a pork chop to each plate and serve.

Braised pork with leeks and bok choy

plenty of protein and B vitamins

Serves 4

1⅓lb (600g) pork tenderloin

2 tbsp (30ml) olive oil

sea salt and black pepper

1 large leek, white part only, thinly sliced

1¼-inch (3cm) piece of gingerroot, peeled and cut into thin sticks

3–4 garlic cloves, peeled and chopped

1¾ cups (400ml) water

¾ cup (200ml) dry white wine or rice wine

2–3 tbsp (30–45ml) light soy sauce, to taste

4 tsp (20ml) superfine sugar, or to taste

2 large heads of bok choy, about 8oz (250g)

Cut the pork into bite-size chunks, trimming away any fat or sinew. Heat a cast-iron or heavy skillet with a little olive oil. Lightly season the pork pieces and brown in batches for about a minute on each side, until golden brown all over. Remove to a plate and set aside.

Add a little more oil to the skillet and stir in the leek, ginger, and garlic. Stir frequently over medium-high heat for 4 to 6 minutes until the leek begins to soften. Add the water, wine, soy sauce, and sugar, scraping the bottom of the pan with a wooden spoon to deglaze.

Return the pork to the pan and stir well. Bring to a boil, then reduce the heat to a simmer. Partially cover the pan with a lid and gently braise for an hour, stirring from time to time, until the pork is very tender and the sauce has reduced by half.

Cut the bok choy into quarters lengthwise and place on top of the pork. Cover the pan with the lid and cook for another 3 to 4 minutes until the bok choy is just tender. Serve the braised pork and vegetables with steamed rice.

Stuffed chicken breasts wrapped in sage and prosciutto

Serves 4

4 large chicken breasts, about 6–7oz (170–200g)

8 sage leaves

5 heaping tbsp (75ml) ricotta

sea salt and black pepper

8 prosciutto slices

4 tsp (20ml) olive oil

handful of thyme sprigs

Cut a deep slit along one side of each chicken breast, without slicing right through, then open it out like a book. On a clean cutting board, mince 4 sage leaves, then mix into the ricotta and season with salt and pepper to taste.

Lay two prosciutto slices on the board, overlapping them slightly. Put a sage leaf in the middle and lay an open chicken breast on top. Spoon a quarter of the ricotta mixture onto the middle of the chicken, then fold the sides together again, to enclose the filling. Now wrap the prosciutto slices around the stuffed chicken breast. Wrap in plastic wrap. Repeat with the rest of the chicken breasts and chill for 1 to 2 hours to firm up slightly.

Heat the oven to 350°F (180°C) and place a roasting pan in the oven to heat up. Heat a heavy skillet and add the olive oil. When hot, pan-fry the prosciutto-wrapped chicken, in batches if necessary, for 2 minutes on each side until browned. Lay a few thyme sprigs on each chicken breast, then place in the hot roasting pan. Cook in the oven for 12 to 15 minutes, depending on size, or until the meat feels just firm when lightly pressed.

Rest the chicken, covered with foil, in a warm place for 5 to 10 minutes. Slice each stuffed breast thickly on the diagonal and arrange on warm plates. Serve with steamed greens and light mashed potatoes or a zesty couscous.

Conchiglie with lamb ragù

Serves 4

3 tbsp (45ml) olive oil

1lb (500g) lean ground lamb

sea salt and black pepper

1 large onion, peeled and minced

2 garlic cloves, peeled and chopped

1 celery stalk, minced

1 large carrot, peeled and minced

1 tbsp (15ml) tomato paste

1 rosemary sprig, leaves only, chopped

few sage leaves, chopped

½ cup (125ml) dry white wine

1½lb (700g) strained tomatoes (passata)

1 cup (250ml) hot water

pinch of sugar (optional)

10oz (300g) dried conchiglie (shells) or other pasta shapes

Heat a large nonstick skillet and add 1 tbsp (15ml) olive oil. When hot, add the ground lamb and some seasoning. Pan-fry, stirring occasionally, for 8 to 10 minutes until browned. Tip into a colander set over a large bowl to drain off the excess oil.

Meanwhile, heat the remaining oil in a large cast-iron pan. Add the onion, garlic, celery, and carrot and cook, stirring, over high heat for 4 to 6 minutes until lightly golden brown. Stir in the tomato paste and cook for another 2 minutes. Add the chopped herbs and pour in the wine, stirring and scraping the bottom of the pan to deglaze. Let the wine simmer until it has reduced to a syrupy glaze.

Add the browned lamb, strained tomatoes, and hot water. Stir well and bring to a low simmer. Partially cover the pan with a lid and simmer for 1 to 1½ hours until the lamb is tender, giving the mixture a stir every now and then. Taste and adjust the seasoning, adding a pinch of sugar if necessary to balance the acidity of the tomatoes. (If preparing in advance, the ragù can now be cooled down and chilled or frozen.)

When ready to serve, bring a pot of salted water to a boil. Add the pasta and boil according to the package directions, until al dente. Drain and immediately toss with a drizzle of olive oil. Divide between warm bowls and spoon over the lamb ragù to serve.

Calves liver with caramelized onions

liver is rich in iron and B vitamins

Serves 4

²/₃lb (350g) calves liver

1 heaping tbsp (15ml) all-purpose flour

sea salt and black pepper

1–2 tbsp (15–30ml) olive oil

small handful of Italian parsley, chopped

Caramelized onions:

2 sweet onions, peeled and thinly sliced

2 tbsp (30ml) olive oil

pinch of superfine sugar

splash of balsamic vinegar

Lemon cornmeal:

7oz (200g) instant cornmeal

generous 2 cups (550ml) milk

generous 2 cups (550ml) chicken stock (see page 249)

2 tbsp (30ml) crème fraîche

finely grated rind of 1 lemon

2 tbsp (30ml) lemon juice, or to taste

Cook the onions first. Heat the olive oil in a pan and add the onions with a little seasoning. Cover and sweat for 6 to 8 minutes, stirring occasionally, until soft. Remove the lid and increase the heat. Stir in the sugar and cook, stirring frequently, until the onions are golden brown. Add a splash of balsamic vinegar and let bubble until well reduced and the pan is quite dry. Keep warm.

Make the cornmeal next. Heat the milk and stock in a large pan with some seasoning. When it begins to simmer, gradually add the cornmeal, whisking constantly to prevent lumps forming. Simmer and stir for about 5 minutes. Take off the heat and stir in the crème fraîche, lemon rind, and juice. Check the seasoning. Cover and keep warm while you prepare the liver.

Trim the liver, peeling away the membrane if necessary. Cut into ½-inch (1cm) thick slices, prising out larger tubes with the knife tip. Mix the flour with a pinch each of salt and pepper on a plate. Coat the liver slices in the seasoned flour.

Cook the liver in batches. Heat a large nonstick skillet over high heat. Add the olive oil, then pan-fry a few slices of liver for about 40 seconds on each side until nicely browned, but still pink in the middle. Remove to a warm plate and repeat to cook the rest, adding a little more oil if needed.

Give the cornmeal a stir and spoon onto warm plates. Top with the caramelized onions and pan-fried liver. Sprinkle over some chopped parsley and serve at once.

Baked zucchini
and wild mushroom
risotto

Serves 4

4 zucchini

sea salt and black pepper

2 large garlic cloves, peeled and thinly sliced

few basil sprigs, leaves only

2–3 tbsp (30–45ml) olive oil, plus extra to drizzle

squeeze of lemon juice

generous 2–2 ½ cups (550–600ml) vegetable or chicken stock (see pages 248–9)

scant 1 cup (200g) risotto rice such as carnaroli, arborio, or vialone nano

generous ⅓ cup (100ml) dry white wine

7oz (200g) wild mushrooms, cleaned and halved or sliced if large

2–3 tbsp (30–45ml) finely grated Parmesan

Heat the oven to 400°F (200°C) and line a large baking sheet with foil. Halve the zucchini lengthwise and score the flesh in a crisscross pattern. Arrange cut side up on the sheet. Season lightly and sprinkle over the garlic slices and basil leaves. Drizzle with olive oil and squeeze over a little lemon juice. Bake for 30 to 40 minutes until the zucchini are soft. Let them cool slightly, then roughly chop the flesh.

For the risotto, bring the stock to a simmer in a pan. Heat another medium pan and add 1 tbsp (15ml) olive oil. Stir in the rice and cook, stirring, for a minute. Pour in the wine and let it bubble to reduce down until the pan is quite dry. Now add the stock, a ladleful at a time, stirring frequently. Let the rice absorb most of the stock in the pan before adding another ladleful.

When the rice is al dente, stir in the chopped zucchini and turn off the heat. Let the risotto stand for a few minutes.

Meanwhile, heat a wide skillet and add 1 to 2 tbsp (15 to 30ml) olive oil. Tip in the mushrooms, season, and toss over high heat for 3 to 4 minutes until they are golden brown and any moisture released has been cooked off. Mix the mushrooms into the risotto, adding a little more boiling stock if you prefer a "wet risotto." Stir in most of the Parmesan and adjust the seasoning.

Divide the risotto among warm plates and sprinkle over the remaining Parmesan to serve.

Grilled provençal vegetable salad

serve with couscous, or as a side dish with broiled fish or meat

Serves 4

1 large zucchini, trimmed

1 medium eggplant, trimmed

1 sweet red pepper

1 sweet yellow pepper

2 garlic cloves, peeled and finely crushed

1 tsp (5ml) herbes de Provence

2 tbsp (30ml) olive oil

sea salt and black pepper

1 tbsp (15ml) balsamic vinegar

extra-virgin olive oil, to drizzle

1–2 tbsp (15–30ml) toasted pine nuts

few basil leaves, torn

Cut the zucchini and eggplant into ¼-inch (½cm) thick slices. Halve, core, and seed the peppers, then cut into slices and place in a bowl with the other vegetables.

Stir the garlic, herbs, olive oil, and seasoning together in a bowl. Drizzle over the vegetables and toss well to coat.

Heat a large griddle or heavy skillet until hot. Griddle the vegetables until they are tender, basting frequently and turning halfway through cooking. The peppers and zucchini will take about 4 to 5 minutes; the eggplants will need 6 to 8 minutes.

Arrange the vegetables on a warm serving platter and drizzle over the balsamic vinegar and extra-virgin olive oil. Sprinkle over the pine nuts and torn basil. Serve warm or at room temperature.

Braised eggplant
Szechuan-style

Serves 4

2 medium eggplants, trimmed

4 tbsp (60ml) sunflower oil

1¼-inch (3cm) piece of gingerroot, peeled and minced

2 garlic cloves, peeled and minced

1 large onion, peeled and roughly chopped

1 red chile, trimmed, seeded, and minced

1 sweet red pepper, cored, seeded, and chopped

sea salt and black pepper

2 green onions, trimmed and thinly sliced on the diagonal

1 tbsp (15ml) toasted sesame seeds, to garnish

Sauce:

⅔ cup (150ml) vegetable or chicken stock (see pages 248–9)

2 tbsp (30ml) light soy sauce

2 tbsp (30ml) rice wine

2 tsp (10ml) Worcestershire sauce

2 tsp (10ml) superfine sugar, or to taste

1½ tsp (7ml) cornstarch

Cut the eggplants into ⅝-inch (1½cm) slices, then halve the slices to give half-moons.

For the sauce, mix all the ingredients together in a small bowl and set aside.

Heat a large pan and add half the oil. Tip in the ginger, garlic, onion, and chile and stir-fry over medium heat for 4 to 5 minutes until the onion begins to soften. Stir in the red pepper and cook for another minute before adding the remaining oil and the eggplant pieces. Season lightly and cook, turning frequently, for 3 to 4 minutes.

Give the sauce a stir and pour into the pan. Stir well, then turn the heat to low. Simmer for 8 to 10 minutes or until the eggplant is just tender, giving the mixture a stir every now and then.

Transfer to a serving dish and sprinkle over the green onions and sesame seeds. Serve with bowls of steamed rice or Asian noodles.

Penne primavera

delicately flavored spring vegetables and pasta

10oz (300g) dried penne or other pasta shapes

sea salt and black pepper

8–10 baby leeks, white part only

4 baby fennel, trimmed

8 radishes, trimmed and halved lengthwise

6 baby carrots, scrubbed or peeled

4 baby turnips, scrubbed and halved

4 baby zucchini, trimmed and thickly sliced on the diagonal

few thyme sprigs

3–4 tbsp (45–60ml) extra-virgin olive oil

juice of ½ lemon

handful of basil leaves, shredded

handful of mint leaves, shredded

3–4 tbsp (45–60ml) freshly grated Parmesan, to serve (optional)

For the pasta, bring a pot of salted water to a boil. At the same time, bring a large pan of water (that will take a large steamer basket) to a boil ready to steam the vegetables. Put all the baby vegetables into your steamer basket and sprinkle over the thyme sprigs and a little sea salt.

Set the steamer basket over the pan of boiling water. Cover and steam for 6 to 8 minutes until the vegetables are just tender.

Meanwhile, add the pasta to the boiling salted water and cook until al dente, according to the package directions. Reserving a little water in the pan, drain the pasta into a colander then tip back into the pan and immediately toss with the olive oil and lemon juice.

When cooked, add the vegetables to the pasta, discarding the thyme sprigs. Toss to mix and season well to taste. Mix through the shredded herbs and divide between warm serving plates. Serve as is, or with a sprinkling of grated Parmesan.

Moroccan spiced pumpkin and lima bean pot

Serves 4

2lb (1kg) wedge of cooking pumpkin (about 1½lb/750g peeled weight)

4 tbsp (60ml) olive oil

1 banana shallot (or 3 regular ones), peeled and chopped

2 garlic cloves, peeled and minced

sea salt and black pepper

1 tsp (5ml) paprika

1 tsp (5ml) ground ginger

1 tsp (5ml) ground cumin

1 tsp (5ml) ground turmeric

2–2½ cups (500–600ml) hot chicken stock (see page 249)

2 x 14oz (398g) cans lima beans, rinsed and drained

bunch of Italian parsley, chopped

bunch of cilantro, chopped

4 tbsp (60ml) plain yogurt, to serve

Remove the skin from the pumpkin, discard the seeds, and roughly chop the flesh into 2-inch (5cm) cubes. Heat half the olive oil in a large pan and add the pumpkin, shallot, garlic, and some seasoning. Stir over high heat for 10 minutes until the pumpkin cubes are lightly caramelized and soft. Add the spices and stir over the heat for another couple of minutes.

Pour in the stock to cover the pumpkin and bring to a simmer. Cook for 10 minutes, then remove from the heat and let cool slightly. While still hot, purée the mixture in a blender until smooth and creamy. (You may need to do this in two batches.)

Return the purée to the pan and bring to a simmer. Tip in the lima beans and chopped herbs. Place over medium heat for 2 to 3 minutes until the beans are hot. Taste and adjust the seasoning.

Ladle the soup into warm bowls and add a spoonful of yogurt. Serve with plenty of warm flat breads.

Note For a lighter version of this soup, as illustrated, use one can of lima beans rather than two.

Healthy kids

Lunchbox dips and dunkers

Serves 4–6

Smoked mackerel pâté:

8oz (250g) smoked mackerel fillets

2 tbsp (30ml) horseradish cream

5 tbsp (75ml) reduced-fat crème fraîche

2 tbsp (30ml) lemon juice, or to taste

freshly ground black pepper

Minted chickpea purée:

14oz (398g) can chickpeas, rinsed and drained

4 tbsp (60ml) plain yogurt

2 tbsp (30ml) lemon juice, or to taste

sea salt and black pepper

handful of mint leaves, chopped

To serve:

raw vegetable sticks, such as carrots, celery, cucumber, sweet red and yellow peppers

cooked shelled shrimp tossed with a drizzle of olive oil and thyme (optional)

To make the fish pâté, flake the smoked mackerel, checking for pin-bones, and place in a food processor. Pulse a few times to break the fish apart. Add half the horseradish cream, crème fraîche, lemon juice, and some black pepper (you won't need to add salt) and pulse again until smooth. Taste the mixture and add more horseradish cream, crème fraîche, and lemon juice until you are happy with the flavor and seasoning. Spoon the mixture into a lunchbox or plastic container and chill.

For the chickpea purée, put the chickpeas, yogurt, lemon juice, and some seasoning into a food processor. Blend until smooth. Transfer the mixture to a bowl and taste for seasoning, adding more lemon juice, salt, and pepper as necessary. Stir through the chopped mint and chill in a lunchbox or plastic container.

Pack a selection of raw vegetable sticks in a separate container to serve with the dips. If liked, pack some shrimp in another container. Add some breadsticks or pita bread, too. Follow with fresh fruit or yogurt.

Note The lunch must be packed in an insulated cooler bag with ice blocks to keep it chilled, especially if shrimp are included.

Crusted fish fillets
with tomato ketchup

a healthy alternative to fish fingers

Serves 4

4 thick, skinless cod fillets, about
4½–4¾oz (130–140g) each

1 cup (50g) fresh white bread crumbs

finely grated rind of 1 lemon

1oz (25g) Parmesan, freshly grated

1–2 thyme sprigs, leaves stripped

sea salt and black pepper

1–2 tbsp (15–30ml) olive oil

lemon wedges, to serve

homemade ketchup (see page 125)

Heat the oven to 425°F (220°C). Check the cod fillets carefully for pin-bones, removing any that you come across with kitchen tweezers. Place the fillets, skinned side up, on a lightly oiled baking sheet.

In a bowl, mix together the bread crumbs, lemon rind, Parmesan, thyme, and a little salt and pepper to taste. Stir in a little olive oil to combine.

Spread the bread crumb mixture evenly on top of each fish fillet. Bake in the oven for 7 to 8 minutes until the topping is golden brown and crisp, and the fish flesh is opaque.

Transfer the fish to warm plates and add a lemon wedge, for squeezing. Serve with homemade ketchup, mashed potatoes, and peas or broccoli.

Turkey brochettes
with red pepper salsa

skinless turkey breast is one of the leanest meats you can buy

Serves 4–5

1lb (500g) boneless skinless turkey breasts

sea salt and black pepper

2 red onions, peeled

1 sweet yellow pepper

1 sweet orange pepper

olive oil, to brush

Marinade:

1 tbsp (15ml) lime juice

1 tbsp (15ml) olive oil

½ tsp (2ml) smoked paprika

½ tsp (2ml) celery salt

½ tsp (2ml) cornstarch

pinch of cayenne pepper

dash of Tabasco sauce (optional)

dash of Worcestershire sauce

Red pepper salsa:

8oz (250g) jar roasted red peppers in olive oil

1 small red onion, peeled and minced

4 green onions, trimmed and minced

handful of cilantro leaves

juice of 1 lime

½ tsp (2ml) honey, to taste

Cut the turkey into 1–1¼-inch (2.5–3cm) cubes. Whisk together all the ingredients for the marinade in a large bowl, adding some salt and pepper. Add the turkey and toss well to coat. Cover with plastic wrap and let marinate in the refrigerator for at least 30 minutes or overnight. Soak 4–5 bamboo skewers in cold water for at least 20 minutes.

Cut the onions into bite-size chunks, similar in size to the turkey cubes. Halve, core, and seed the peppers, then cut into 1–1¼-inch (2.5–3cm) squares. Thread the peppers, onions, and turkey cubes alternately onto the skewers. Place on a lightly oiled sheet, cover with plastic wrap, and chill until ready to cook.

For the salsa, drain the peppers and mince. Place in a bowl and add all the rest of the ingredients. Toss together and season with salt and pepper to taste. (The salsa is now ready to eat, or it can be chilled for up to an hour.)

To cook, heat a stovetop grill pan or the broiler until hot. Brush the brochettes with a little olive oil and cook for 10 to 15 minutes, turning several times. The turkey should feel just firm when lightly pressed; don't overcook or it will be dry. Serve immediately, with the red pepper salsa.

Chicken burgers
with sweet potato wedges

low fat burger and chips

Makes 6 small burgers

3 tbsp (45ml) olive oil

1 medium sweet onion, peeled and minced

2 garlic cloves, peeled and finely crushed

sea salt and black pepper

²/₃lb (350g) ground boneless skinless chicken breasts

1 large egg

handful of herbs, such as Italian parsley and chives, chopped

Sweet potato wedges:

3 medium sweet potatoes, peeled

olive oil, to drizzle

honey, to drizzle (optional)

To serve:

6 mini buns, preferably whole wheat, split

1 large ripe avocado

squeeze of lemon juice

1 large beefsteak tomato, thinly sliced

homemade ketchup (see page 125)

Heat 1 tbsp (15ml) olive oil in a pan and sweat the onion and garlic with seasoning for 4 to 6 minutes until soft but not brown. Tip into a bowl; cool completely.

Add the chicken, egg, and seasoning, then stir in the chopped herbs, until evenly distributed. Cover with plastic wrap and chill for an hour to let the mixture firm up.

Shape the mixture into 6 small patties, with moist hands; try not to compact them. Place on a sheet lined with baking parchment. Chill until ready to cook.

Heat the oven to 400°F (200°C). Line a baking sheet with baking parchment. Cut the sweet potatoes into wedges and place in a large bowl with a drizzle of olive oil and some seasoning. Spread out in a single layer on the baking sheet and bake for 15 to 20 minutes until golden brown at the edges. If you wish, drizzle with a little honey. Keep warm in a low oven.

To cook the burgers, heat 2 tbsp (30ml) olive oil in a large skillet or stovetop grill pan. When hot, pan-fry the patties for 4 minutes on each side until golden brown and just cooked through. (Don't press them with a spatula as they cook or you'll squeeze out the juices.) Remove to a warm plate and let rest.

Lightly toast the buns on both sides. Halve, peel, and pit the avocado, then slice thinly, squeezing over a little lemon juice to prevent them discoloring. Sandwich each bun with a chicken burger and a few slices of avocado and tomato. Serve immediately, with the sweet potato wedges and ketchup.

Stir-fried duck
in lettuce cups

Serves 4–6

1 iceberg lettuce

4 duck breasts, about 6oz (175g) each

¼ tsp (1ml) Szechuan peppercorns

½ tsp (2ml) black peppercorns

½–1 tsp (2–5ml) five-spice powder

pinch of sea salt

olive oil, to drizzle

1 cucumber

2 green onions, trimmed

5–6 tbsp (75–90ml) hoisin sauce

1 tbsp (15ml) sesame seeds, to sprinkle

For the lettuce cups, remove the outer layers from the lettuce until you get 4–6 neat whole leaves. Trim around each leaf with scissors to neaten the edges, so that they resemble cups. Place one on each serving plate.

Remove the skin and fat from the duck breasts, then slice the flesh into thin strips. Put the peppercorns, five-spice powder, and sea salt into a mortar and grind to a powder. Sprinkle this over the duck slices, drizzle with a little olive oil, and toss to coat evenly.

Halve the cucumber and scoop out the seeds, then cut the flesh into finger-length strips. Slice the green onions very finely on the diagonal.

Heat a nonstick wide skillet until hot and you can feel the heat rising above the pan. Add the duck and stir-fry for 2 minutes. Add the green onions and hoisin sauce and toss well to coat. Stir-fry for another minute until the duck is just cooked through. Toss with a handful of cucumber strips.

Divide the stir-fry between the lettuce cups. Sprinkle with the sesame seeds and sprinkle the remaining cucumber strips around each plate. Serve immediately.

Rigatoni with yellow squash and green zucchini

Serves 4–5

8oz (250g) dried rigatoni or other pasta shapes

sea salt and black pepper

2 large green zucchini, trimmed

2 large yellow squash, trimmed

3–4 tbsp (45–60ml) olive oil

1 garlic clove, peeled and finely crushed

handful of basil leaves

Parmesan, to grate

Add the pasta to a pot of boiling salted water and cook according to the package directions until al dente.

Meanwhile, halve the zucchini and squash lengthwise and slice thickly. Heat a large skillet and add the olive oil. Tip in the crushed garlic and sauté for just less than a minute.

Add the zucchini and the squash with a pinch of salt and a grinding of pepper. (If your pan is not large enough, cook in two batches.) Pan-fry over high heat for 3 to 4 minutes until just tender and lightly golden brown around the sides. Take off the heat.

When ready, drain the pasta and immediately toss with the zucchini, squash and basil. Taste and season. Divide among warm plates and grate over some Parmesan to serve.

Baked eggs
with ratatouille

eggs are one of the best sources of protein for children

Serves 4

1 large red onion, peeled

1 small eggplant, trimmed

1 large sweet red pepper, halved, cored, and seeded

1 large sweet green pepper, halved, cored, and seeded

1 large zucchini, trimmed

3–4 tbsp (45–60ml) olive oil

sea salt and black pepper

2 garlic cloves, peeled and minced

¼–½ tsp (1–2ml) mild chili powder (optional)

1 tsp (5ml) ground cumin

1 tsp (5ml) sweet paprika

8oz (250g) canned chopped tomatoes

4 large eggs

Heat the oven to 400°F (200°C). Chop the onion, eggplant, peppers, and zucchini into ⅝-inch (1.5cm) cubes, keeping them separate. Put a large skillet over high heat and add the olive oil, onion, and a little seasoning. Sauté for 2 minutes, then add the eggplant, peppers, and garlic and cook for another minute. Tip in the zucchini and sauté for another minute or two.

Add the ground spices and chopped tomatoes. Bring to a simmer and cook for 8 to 10 minutes until the vegetables are tender. Taste and adjust the seasoning.

Divide the ratatouille between four individual shallow ovenproof dishes. Make an indentation in each portion with the back of a spoon, then crack an egg into each one. Sprinkle the top of each egg with a pinch each of salt and pepper.

Stand the dishes on a large baking sheet and bake for 10 to 12 minutes until the egg whites are set but the yolks are still runny in the middle. Serve immediately, with some whole wheat toasts on the side.

Fromage frais, yogurt, and plum purée ripple

plenty of protein and calcium for strong bones and teeth

Serves 4–6

4 ripe plums, about 1lb (500g)

½ tsp (2ml) ground cinnamon

2–3 tbsp (30–45ml) superfine sugar, to taste

1 star anise (optional)

1¼ cups (300ml) low-fat plain yogurt

1¼ cups (300ml) reduced-fat fromage frais

2–3 tbsp (30–45ml) confectioners' sugar, or to taste

Halve the plums, remove the pits, and roughly chop the flesh. Toss with the cinnamon and 2 tbsp (30ml) superfine sugar. Place a wide skillet over high heat, tip in the plums, and add the star anise if using. Sauté for 4 to 6 minutes until the plums are soft, moistening with a splash of water if necessary. Taste for sweetness, adding more sugar if the plums are too tart. Discard the star anise.

Transfer the cooked plums to a blender or food processor and whiz until smooth. For a really smooth purée, pass through a fine strainer to remove any pulpy bits. Let cool completely.

Spoon the yogurt and fromage frais into a large bowl and add the confectioners' sugar. Beat lightly to mix, then ripple through all but 2 tbsp (30ml) of the plum purée. Spoon into individual glasses or plastic glasses and swirl the remaining plum purée on top. Serve at once.

Healthy entertaining

Mixed fish sashimi

Serves 4–6 as an appetizer

14oz (400g) sashimi-grade swordfish fillet

14oz (400g) sashimi-grade center-cut tuna fillet

10oz (300g) sashimi-grade skinless salmon fillet

1 very fresh mackerel, about 10oz (300g), filleted (optional, see note)

To serve:

light soy sauce

pickled ginger

wasabi paste

Trim off any dark flesh from the swordfish and neaten the edges (you can save all the fish trimmings to make fish cakes). Trim the tuna to a neat log and neaten the edges of the salmon fillet. Carefully check over the salmon and mackerel fillets for pin-bones, removing any you find with kitchen tweezers.

Wrap each fish in plastic wrap and place in the freezer for 45 minutes to let the flesh firm up slightly, making them easier to slice.

Take the fish from the freezer and remove the plastic wrap. Thinly slice each fish with a very sharp knife and overlap the fish slices in neat rows on a serving platter. The sashimi can now be chilled for a few hours until ready to serve. Bring to the table with little dipping bowls of light soy sauce, pickled ginger, and wasabi paste.

Note Only use mackerel if you are able to obtain a freshly caught fish from the sea. Otherwise, use an extra 3½oz (100g) each swordfish, tuna, and salmon.

5 ways with leafy greens

The diversity of greens is astonishing. As a child, I ate lots of kale, which was, and still is, regarded as a humble vegetable, akin to rutabaga and turnip. But like spinach and the once exotic cavalo nero, kale is fantastic in soups and stews, or simply sautéed with a touch of garlic and chile.

The general rule is the darker the color, the richer the nutrients. In addition to fiber, leafy veg provide calcium, magnesium, iron, zinc, folic acid, and the valuable antioxidants—Beta carotene and vitamin C. These are important for boosting the immune system and improving digestion. So, aim to eat a variety of leafy greens through the week, making the most of what is in season.

1

Bruschetta with cavalo nero and prosciutto

Chop 2 bunches (10oz−⅔lb/300−350g) of cavalo nero. Cook 8 slices of prosciutto in a large nonstick skillet until brown and crisp on both sides. Transfer to a plate; set aside. Add 2 tbsp (30ml) olive oil to the pan and 4 unpeeled garlic cloves. Pan-fry for a minute or two to flavor the oil, then add the cavalo nero, some seasoning, and a glass of water. Cook, stirring frequently, for 5 to 6 minutes until the leaves are tender and the water has cooked off. Meanwhile, halve a ciabatta lengthwise, then cut each piece in two and toast lightly. Pile the ham and cavalo nero onto the warm toasts and serve, topped with the garlic. **Serves 4**

2

Purple sprouting broccoli with Thai flavors

Cut 14oz (400g) purple sprouting broccoli into even lengths. For the dressing, mix 1 seeded, minced small red chile with 2 tbsp (30ml) sesame oil, 4 tsp (20ml) fish sauce, the juice of 1 lime and ½−1 tsp (2−5 ml) sugar. Cook the broccoli in a steamer for 4 minutes until tender and bright green. Immediately transfer to a warm plate, spoon over the dressing, sprinkle with 1 tbsp (15ml) toasted sesame seeds and serve. **Serves 4**

3 Spinach with chickpeas and harissa

Drain a 14oz (398g) can of chickpeas, rinse in a strainer, and set aside to drain. In a large skillet, sauté 2 chopped garlic cloves in 2 tbsp (30ml) olive oil over low heat, without browning. Tip in the chickpeas, add 1 tbsp (15ml) harissa and some seasoning, and increase the heat slightly. Stir and cook for 3 to 4 minutes until the chickpeas are warmed through. Stir in 7oz (200g) baby spinach leaves and cook for barely a minute just until the spinach has wilted. Transfer to warm plates and serve immediately. **Serves 2**

4 Bok choy with ginger and garlic

Wash 1lb (500g) bok choy and separate the stalks and leaves, then slice the stalks on the diagonal into bite-size pieces. Chop 1 large garlic clove and a ¾-inch (2cm) piece of gingerroot. Heat a wok until hot, then add 4 tsp (20ml) peanut oil, followed by the garlic and ginger. Stir-fry for a minute, adding the bok choy stalks with a small splash of water as the garlic and ginger begin to color. Add the leaves, 2 tbsp (30ml) oyster sauce, and a few grindings of black pepper. Stir-fry over high heat for another 30 seconds until the bok choy is tender. Transfer to a warm plate and serve. **Serves 4**

5 Kale, chorizo, and potato soup

Trim 7oz (200g) kale, cutting off the hard stems, then mince the leaves and place in a bowl; set aside. Heat 2 tbsp (30ml) olive oil in a large pan and sauté 2 chopped onions and 2 minced garlic cloves for 5 to 6 minutes, stirring frequently, until soft but not browned. Tip in 5oz (150g) diced chorizo sausage, stir, and cook for a few more minutes.

Add 2 diced, scrubbed, large red-skinned potatoes, 6 cups (1.5 liters) water to cover, and some salt and pepper. Stir well and bring to a boil. Lower the heat and simmer for 10 to 12 minutes until the potatoes are just cooked. Tip in the kale and simmer for another 3 to 5 minutes until tender. Check the seasoning and serve in warm bowls. **Serves 4**

Hot and sour clam broth with noodles

delicate flavors, high in nutrients, yet low in fat

Serves 4–6 as an appetizer

Broth:

2-inch (5cm) piece of gingerroot, peeled and sliced into thin sticks

1 lemongrass stalk, trimmed and chopped

2 red chiles, trimmed and sliced

4–5 kaffir lime leaves

3 tbsp (45ml) fish sauce

3 tbsp (45ml) rice wine vinegar

3 tbsp (45ml) light soy sauce

2½ tbsp (40ml) jaggery or brown sugar

juice of 1 lime

6 cups (1.5 liters) fish stock (see page 248)

To serve:

2²/₃lb (1.2kg) fresh clams

1⅓lb (600g) fresh udon noodles

sesame oil, to drizzle

handful of basil or cilantro leaves, torn

Put all the ingredients for the broth into a large pan and bring to a boil, stirring occasionally to help dissolve the sugar. Reduce the heat slightly and simmer for 3 to 4 minutes. Bring another pan of water to a boil for the noodles.

Scrub the clams under cold running water and discard any that do not close tightly when tapped. Increase the heat under the broth pan and slide the clams into the broth. Cover, bring back to a boil, and simmer for 3 to 4 minutes until the shells have opened. Discard any that remain shut.

Meanwhile, add the noodles to the pan of boiling water and cook for about 2 minutes, then tip into a colander and drain well. Immediately toss with a drizzle of sesame oil and divide among warm bowls. Ladle over the clams and hot broth. Sprinkle over some torn basil or cilantro and serve.

Chilled leek and avocado soup

ideal for summer entertaining

Serves 4 as an appetizer

2 tbsp (30ml) olive oil

8oz (250g) leeks, white part only, minced

1 onion, peeled and minced

sea salt and black pepper

splash of dry white wine

1 medium potato, about 5oz (150g), peeled and chopped

bouquet garni (thyme sprig, bay leaf, and a few parsley stalks, tied together)

3¼ cups (750ml) vegetable or chicken stock (see pages 248–9)

1 large ripe avocado

juice of ½ lemon, or to taste

Heat the olive oil in a large pan and add the leeks, onion, and some seasoning. Stir, then cover and let the vegetables sweat over low heat for 5 minutes until softened.

Remove the lid, turn up the heat slightly, and add a splash of wine. Let bubble until reduced down to a syrupy glaze. Stir in the potato and add the bouquet garni. Pour in the stock and bring to a boil. Season with salt and pepper, then cover and let simmer for 10 to 15 minutes until the potato is soft. Discard the bouquet garni.

Halve the avocado, remove the pit, and scoop out the flesh into a blender. Ladle in half of the soup liquor and vegetables and blend to a smooth purée. Tip into a large bowl, or for a really smooth soup, push the purée through a fine strainer into the bowl. Blend the remaining liquor and vegetables until smooth and add to the rest of the soup. Stir and adjust the seasoning, adding salt, pepper, and a little lemon juice to taste.

Let the soup cool, then chill for a few hours or overnight. Pour into chilled bowls to serve.

Baby spinach, artichoke, and watercress salad

packed with vitamins and minerals

10oz (300g) baby spinach leaves

7oz (200g) watercress, trimmed of stalks

10oz (280g) jar grilled artichoke halves in olive oil

1 unwaxed lemon

Parmesan shavings, to serve

Dressing:

1 garlic clove, peeled

sea salt and black pepper

1 tbsp (15ml) whole grain mustard

4 tsp (20ml) cider vinegar

4 tbsp (60ml) extra-virgin olive oil

2 tbsp (30ml) walnut oil

For the dressing, finely crush the garlic with a pinch each of salt and pepper, using a large mortar and pestle. Stir in the mustard, cider vinegar, olive oil, and walnut oil. Taste and adjust the seasoning.

Wash the spinach and watercress leaves, pat dry, and place in a large salad bowl. Drain the artichoke hearts and pat with paper towels to absorb the excess oil. Cut each artichoke half in two and add to the salad leaves. Finely grate the rind from the lemon over the salad and add a handful of Parmesan shavings.

Toss the salad with the dressing just as you are ready to serve. Divide between serving plates and sprnkle over a few more Parmesan shavings if you wish.

195

Seared scallops
with minted peas and fava beans

Serves 4

24 king scallops, shelled and cleaned

coarse sea salt

2½ cups (250g) shelled peas, thawed if frozen

2 cups (300g) shelled fava beans, thawed if frozen

2 thyme sprigs, leaves only

1–2 tbsp (15–30ml) olive oil

small piece of butter

handful of mint, leaves roughly chopped

extra-virgin olive oil, to drizzle

Take the scallops from the refrigerator and set aside while you cook the vegetables. Bring a pan of salted water to a boil, tip in the peas, and blanch for 3 to 4 minutes or until tender. Scoop them out with a slotted spoon and plunge into a bowl of iced water to refresh. Drain well and tip into a bowl.

Return the water to a boil and blanch the fava beans for 3 to 4 minutes or until tender. Drain well, refresh in iced water, and drain again. Gently squeeze the fava beans to pop them out of their skins. Add to the peas and set aside.

Put the thyme leaves on a board and sprinkle with 1 tsp (5ml) coarse sea salt. Mince, then sprinkle the thyme salt over one side of the scallops. Heat a griddle or large skillet and add the olive oil.

Pan-fry the scallops for 1½ minutes on each side, depending on thickness—they should feel slightly springy when pressed. Make sure you turn them in the same order you put them into the pan to ensure even cooking. Remove to a warm plate and rest for a minute while you reheat the vegetables.

Tip the peas and fava beans into the skillet and add a splash of water and a little butter. Heat for a minute to warm through, season to taste, and toss through the mint leaves.

Spoon the vegetables onto warm plates and top with the scallops. Sprinkle with a little more thyme salt if you wish. Drizzle a little extra-virgin olive oil around each plate and serve immediately.

Red mullet
with orange and fennel en papillote

Serves 4

8 red mullet fillets, about 3½oz (100g) each

2 large oranges

1 large or 2 medium heads of fennel

2 red chiles

2 tsp (10ml) fennel seeds

olive oil, to drizzle

4 splashes of dry white wine

Heat the oven to 400°F (200°C). Cut 4 large squares of baking parchment. Fold each square in half to form a crease in the middle, then open out and set aside. Check the red mullet fillets for pin-bones, removing any with kitchen tweezers.

To prepare the oranges, slice off the top and bottom, then cut off the peel and pith following the curve of the fruit. Now, holding the orange over a strainer set on top of a bowl to catch the juice, cut along the membranes to release each segment. Squeeze out any juice from the pulp and discard.

Trim the fennel, then slice thinly. Halve, seed, and thinly slice the chiles into rings.

Divide the fennel slices, orange segments, and chile slices among the parchment squares, piling them on one side of the crease. Lay two red mullet fillets on each pile. Sprinkle over the fennel seeds and drizzle with a little olive oil. Fold the other side of the parchment over the filling to enclose.

To seal each package, make small folds all along the edges to hold them together. Just before the final fold, tilt the package slightly and pour in a splash of wine and a quarter of the orange juice. Repeat with the remaining packages.

Place the packages on two large baking sheets and bake for 10 minutes until the fish is just firm, opaque, and cooked through. Put a package on each warm plate and bring to the table to cut open.

peppers are packed with
immune-boosting antioxidants

Saffron-marinated bream with sweet and sour peppers

Serves 4

4 black bream fillets, about 5oz (150g) each

2½ tbsp (38ml) olive oil

generous pinch of saffron strands

sea salt and black pepper

basil sprigs, to garnish

Sweet and sour peppers:

6 sweet red peppers

2 tbsp (30ml) olive oil

1 tsp (5ml) superfine sugar

small splash of red wine vinegar

Trim the bream fillets to neaten and pull out any pin-bones with kitchen tweezers. Mix the olive oil and saffron strands together in a wide dish. Add the fish fillets and toss well to coat. Grind over some pepper, cover with plastic wrap, and let marinate in the refrigerator for 20 minutes.

To prepare the peppers, halve, core, and seed, then cut into thin slices. Heat the olive oil in a large skillet or wok, add the peppers, and stir-fry over high heat for 2 to 3 minutes until they begin to soften. Season with salt and pepper and add the sugar and a small splash of wine vinegar. Let bubble for a minute or two until the vinegar has cooked down and the peppers are tender. Take off the heat and set aside; keep warm.

To cook the fish, heat a wide nonstick skillet until hot. Season the bream fillets with salt and pepper and pan-fry, skin side down, for about 2 minutes until the skin is golden brown and crisp. Flip the fillets over and pan-fry the other side for a minute until the flesh is opaque.

Divide the peppers between warm plates and top with the bream fillets. Serve immediately, garnished with basil.

Glazed salmon
with bok choy and shiitake

Serves 4

4 skinless salmon fillets, cut from the thick end, about 5oz (150g) each

Marinade:

2 tbsp (30ml) miso paste

1 tbsp (15ml) mirin

4 tsp (20ml) sesame oil

1½ tsp (7ml) sake

1½ tsp (7ml) light soy sauce

1 tbsp (15ml) superfine sugar or honey

freshly ground black pepper

Bok choy and shiitake:

1lb (500g) bok choy, washed and drained

7oz (200g) shiitake mushrooms, cleaned and stalks removed

1 tbsp (15ml) peanut oil

1 garlic clove, peeled and minced

finger-length piece of gingerroot, peeled and finely shredded

sea salt and black pepper

1 tbsp (15ml) light soy sauce

1 tbsp (15ml) fish sauce

2 tsp (10ml) rice wine vinegar

1 tbsp (15ml) sesame seeds, to sprinkle

Check the salmon fillets for pin-bones, removing any you find with kitchen tweezers. Mix all the marinade ingredients together in a small bowl to make a paste and spread this all over each fillet to coat. Place the fillets in a wide dish, cover with plastic wrap, and let marinate in the refrigerator for at least 30 minutes, preferably overnight.

Trim the bok choy, cutting off the base to separate the individual leaves. Cut off the green leaves and set aside; finely shred the stalks. Cut off the woody stalks from the shiitake mushrooms, then slice thickly.

Heat the oven to 425°F (220°C). Place the salmon fillets on a nonstick or lightly oiled baking sheet and bake for 5 to 7 minutes until cooked around the edges but still medium rare in the center. The fillets should feel slightly springy when pressed. Transfer to a warm plate and rest in a warm place.

Meanwhile, to cook the vegetables, heat the oil in a wok or large skillet over medium heat. Tip in the garlic and ginger and stir-fry for a minute until golden. Add the mushrooms, season lightly, and stir-fry for about 2 minutes until any juices released have been cooked off. Add the bok choy leaves and stalks followed by the soy sauce, fish sauce, and rice wine vinegar. Stir-fry for another minute until the bok choy has just wilted.

Pile the stir-fry onto warm plates. Break the salmon fillets into large flakes and arrange on top. Add a sprinkling of sesame seeds and serve, with bowls of steamed rice.

Stir-fried duck with noodles

quick and easy special stir-fry for two

Serves 2

2 skinless duck breasts, about 5oz (150g) each, trimmed

1 garlic clove, peeled and finely grated

1¼-inch (3cm) piece of gingerroot, peeled and finely grated

1 tsp (5ml) five-spice powder

sea salt and black pepper

3 tbsp (45ml) oyster sauce

1 tbsp (15ml) dark soy sauce

½ tsp (2ml) cornstarch, mixed with 2 tbsp (30ml) water

2 portions of dried noodles, such as thin udon or Chinese egg noodles about 2½oz (65g) each

sesame oil, to drizzle

1–2 tbsp (15–30ml) olive oil

1 long red chile, trimmed and sliced on the diagonal

2 heads of bok choy, leaves separated

3 green onions, trimmed and chopped

grated rind of 1 lime, plus a squeeze of juice

Slice the duck breasts thickly and toss with the grated garlic, ginger, five-spice powder, and a little salt and pepper. Stir the oyster sauce, soy sauce, and cornstarch mixture together in a small bowl.

For the noodles, bring a pot of water to a boil. Add the noodles and cook for 2 minutes less than the suggested time (on the package directions). Drain well and immediately toss with a drizzle of sesame oil.

Heat a wok or large nonstick skillet and add a little olive oil. When hot, add the duck fillets and pan-fry over high heat for 1 to 1½ minutes until golden brown around the edges but not completely cooked through. Remove to a plate and set aside.

Add a little more oil to the pan and tip in the chile and bok choy. Stir-fry for a minute, then pour in the sauce mixture. Bring to a simmer, then return the duck to the pan and cook for another minute. The sauce should begin to thicken.

Add the noodles and green onions to the pan. Toss over the heat until the noodles are warmed through. Squeeze over a little lime juice and serve immediately, sprinkled with grated lime rind.

Guinea fowl with pea and lettuce fricassée

lean, succulent white meat and quick-braised vegetables

Serves 4

4 boneless guinea fowl breasts, about 4½oz (130g) each

sea salt and black pepper

4 tsp (20ml) olive oil

few thyme sprigs, plus extra to garnish

Pea and lettuce fricassée:

small piece of butter

1lb (500g) shelled peas, thawed if frozen

few thyme sprigs

splash of water or chicken stock (see page 249)

3–4 iceberg lettuce leaves, shredded

Trim the guinea fowl breasts to neaten and season with a little salt and pepper. Heat a wide skillet and add a little olive oil. Add the guinea fowl breasts, skin side down, with the thyme sprigs and pan-fry for about 4 to 5 minutes until the skin is golden brown and crisp.

Turn the breasts and cook on the other side for about 2 minutes. They should feel very slightly springy when pressed and should be succulent and slightly pink inside. Transfer to a warm plate and set aside to rest in a warm place while you make the fricassée.

Melt the butter in a pan and tip in the peas with some seasoning. Add the thyme sprigs and a splash of water or stock and braise the peas for 3 to 4 minutes until tender and the pan is almost dry. Toss in the shredded lettuce and cook for another minute until the leaves have just wilted. Taste and adjust the seasoning.

Divide the fricassée among warm plates and rest a guinea fowl breast on top. Serve at once, garnished with thyme. Accompany with new potatoes if you like.

Honey-glazed partridge with mashed rutabagas and cabbage

Serves 2

2 oven-ready partridges, about 10oz (300g) each

sea salt and black pepper

2 tbsp (30ml) olive oil

6 garlic cloves (unpeeled)

few rosemary sprigs

few thyme sprigs

2–3 tbsp (30–45ml) honey

Mashed rutabagas:

1 large rutabaga, about 1¼lb (550g)

1 tbsp (15ml) butter

Sautéed cabbage:

½ head of savoy cabbage, core removed and shredded

4 tsp (20ml) olive oil

squeeze of lemon juice, to taste

For the mashed rutabagas, peel the rutabaga and cut into 1¼–1½-inch (3–4cm) chunks. Cook in salted water to cover for 15 minutes until quite soft. Meanwhile, blanch the cabbage in a pan of salted water for 2 to 3 minutes. Drain and refresh under cold running water; drain and set aside.

Drain the rutabaga and return to the pan. Add the butter and crush with a potato masher, seasoning with a little more salt and pepper to taste. (For a smooth mash, whiz in a food processor, then return to the pan.)

Season the partridges and heat up a skillet. When hot, add the olive oil, garlic, rosemary, and thyme. Sear the partridges for 1½ to 2 minutes on each side until nicely browned. Drizzle the honey over the birds and add a good splash of water to the pan. Cook, basting frequently, for 6 to 8 minutes until the partridge breasts feel slightly springy when pressed, indicating that they're medium rare. Transfer to a warm plate and rest for a few minutes while you reheat the vegetables.

Warm up the mashed rutabagas, giving the mixture a few stirs. For the cabbage, heat the olive oil in a pan, then add the blanched cabbage and toss until piping hot. Adjust the seasoning with salt, pepper, and a little lemon juice.

Pile the mashed rutabagas and sautéed cabbage onto warm plates and sit the braised partridges alongside. Serve immediately.

Roasted pigeon
with pickled red cabbage

Serves 4

4 oven-ready wood pigeons, about
10oz (280g) each

4 tsp (20ml) olive oil

sea salt and black pepper

small piece of butter

Pickled red cabbage:

1 red cabbage, about 1¾lb (850g)

2 tbsp (30ml) butter

¼ cup (50g) brown sugar

4 tbsp (60ml) red wine or malt vinegar

To prepare the cabbage, quarter and cut out the tough core, then finely shred the leaves and place in a bowl. Melt the butter in a large, wide pan and add the sugar and vinegar with a little splash of water. Stir until the sugar has dissolved, then add the shredded cabbage and toss to coat. Cover and braise for 45 minutes to 1 hour until the cabbage is tender, lifting the lid to give it a stir every once in a while.

Heat the oven to 375°F (190°C). Aim to cook the pigeons about 20 minutes before the cabbage will be ready. Heat a wide ovenproof pan and add a little olive oil. Season the pigeons inside and out with salt and pepper. Add to the hot pan and pan-fry for about 2 minutes on each side until evenly browned all over. Add a piece of butter, turn the pigeons breast upward, and spoon the foaming butter over them to baste.

Transfer the pan to the oven and roast for another 8 to 10 minutes to finish cooking the pigeons—the breasts should feel slightly springy when pressed, indicating that they are medium rare. Remove from the oven and rest in a warm place for 5 to 10 minutes.

To serve, pile the pickled red cabbage onto warm serving plates and place a roasted pigeon alongside.

packed with protein, iron, and vitamin C

Pot-roast sirloin of beef with root vegetables

Serves 4

2¼lb (1.2kg) beef sirloin

2–3 tbsp (30–45ml) all-purpose flour

sea salt and black pepper

2 large carrots, peeled and halved lengthwise

1 rutabaga, peeled

1 large kohlrabi, peeled

2 large leeks, trimmed

4 tbsp (60ml) olive oil

1 head of garlic, halved horizontally

²/₃ cup (150ml) red wine

1¼ cups (300ml) beef or chicken stock (see page 249)

handful of thyme sprigs

handful of rosemary sprigs

1 tsp (5ml) black peppercorns

1 tsp (5ml) coriander seeds

Heat the oven to 350°F (180°C). Trim off any excess fat and sinew from the beef. Mix the flour with a generous pinch each of salt and pepper on a wide plate. Roll the beef in the seasoned flour to coat, shaking or patting off any excess. Set aside.

Cut all the vegetables into large chunks. Put a large cast-iron casserole or heavy pan over medium-high heat. Add a thin layer of olive oil and tip in the carrots, rutabaga, and a little seasoning. Cook for 4 to 5 minutes, stirring frequently, until golden brown. With a slotted spoon, transfer to a colander set over a large bowl to drain off any oil. Next, cook the kohlrabi, leeks, and garlic, with a little more oil if necessary. Add to the colander.

Sear the beef in the hot pan, adding a little more oil if necessary, for 8 to 9 minutes until evenly browned all over. Transfer to a plate and set aside. Pour the red wine into the pan, stirring to deglaze, and let bubble until reduced by two-thirds. Stir in the stock. Return the beef and any juices released to the pan.

Spoon the vegetables around the beef and add the herbs, peppercorns, and coriander seeds. Cover with a lid and transfer to the oven. Cook for about 25 to 30 minutes for medium-rare beef. Transfer the beef to a platter, cover with foil, and let rest in a warm place for about 15 minutes.

Just before carving, spoon the vegetables onto a serving platter and keep warm. The sauce will be quite thin; to thicken it if required, boil to reduce slightly, then pass through a fine strainer into a warm pitcher. Thinly slice the beef and add to the platter. Serve with rustic bread and a side salad if you wish.

Seared veal tenderloin with Jerusalem artichoke purée

Serves 4

1½lb (800g) veal tenderloin

4 tsp–2 tbsp (20–30ml) olive oil

sea salt and black pepper

Artichoke purée:

1⅓lb (600g) Jerusalem artichokes, sliced

2 cups (500ml) water or vegetable stock
(see page 248)

small piece of butter

For the purée, put the Jerusalem artichokes into a pan with some salt and pepper and pour in the water or stock to cover. Bring to a simmer and cook for about 15 to 20 minutes until very soft. Drain the artichokes, reserving the cooking liquor.

Tip the artichokes into a food processor and add the butter. Blend for a few minutes until smooth, adding a splash of the liquor as necessary to get the right texture. You'll need to stop the machine to scrape down the sides once or twice. Push the purée through a strainer back into the pan and season.

Heat the oven to 400°F (200°C). Cut any sinew off the veal and trim the edges to neaten so that the veal is evenly thick throughout. Rub all over with olive oil and season with salt and pepper. Heat a wide ovenproof skillet until hot. Add a little oil to the pan and sear the veal tenderloin for about 2 minutes on each side until browned all over.

Transfer the skillet to the oven and cook for 20 minutes or until the veal is medium rare—it should feel springy when pressed. Transfer to a warm platter, cover with foil, and rest for 5 to 10 minutes while you reheat the artichoke purée.

Carve the veal into thick slices and overlap them on warm serving plates. Pour any juices from the platter into the hot pan, then drizzle over each plate. Serve with the Jerusalem artichoke purée, and purple sprouting broccoli if you wish.

veal is low in fat, yet high in protein

Lamb steaks
with Puy lentils and green beans

Serves 4

4 lamb leg steaks, about 7oz (220g) each

few thyme sprigs

few rosemary sprigs

1 tsp (5ml) coriander seeds, lightly crushed

1 tsp (5ml) black peppercorns, lightly crushed

1 tbsp (15ml) olive oil

sea salt

Lentils and green beans:

1¼ cups (250g) Puy lentils

few thyme sprigs

few rosemary sprigs

½ head of garlic, cut horizontally

3⅓ cups (800ml) chicken stock (see page 249)

10oz (300g) green beans

splash of balsamic vinegar

Trim the lamb of any sinew, then place in a wide dish with the herbs, coriander seeds, peppercorns, and olive oil. Toss to coat the meat and let marinate in the refrigerator for at least a few hours, preferably overnight.

To cook the lentils, put them in a pan with the herbs and garlic, then pour on the stock. Bring to a boil, lower the heat, and simmer for 15 to 20 minutes until tender. Drain the lentils, reserving the stock; discard the garlic and herb sprigs.

Blanch the beans in a pan of salted water for 3 to 5 minutes until tender. Drain and refresh in a bowl of iced water, then drain again. Set aside.

Heat the oven to 375°F (190°C). Sprinkle the lamb with a little salt and sear in a hot ovenproof pan for 2 to 3 minutes. Turn over and cook the other side for 2 minutes until browned. Transfer the pan to the oven and roast for 6 to 8 minutes until medium rare— the lamb will be slightly springy when pressed. Transfer to a warm plate and pat with paper towels to absorb the excess fat. Cover with foil and let rest for 5 minutes.

Meanwhile, pour off most of the fat from the pan and tip in the lentils and beans. Add a splash of balsamic vinegar, a little of the reserved stock, and some seasoning. Toss over high heat for a few minutes to warm the beans and lentils through.

Spoon the lentils and beans onto warm serving plates. Thickly slice the lamb and arrange on top. Drizzle over any remaining pan juices and serve.

energize... exercise

An active lifestyle has been important to me over the years. I played soccer when I was younger and, for the past 8 years, I've become obsessed with running and trying out various water sports and skiing. However, like many people, during a stressful period in my life I fell into a self-destructive pattern, which included comfort eating and living a sedentary lifestyle. Now that I'm back to exercising regularly, I cannot emphasize enough the value of being active. Apart from the initial benefit of losing weight in my case, regular exercise strengthens the most important muscle of all— the heart. It's also fantastic for relieving stress, something I'm definitely in need of.

A common excuse I know, but finding time to exercise is my biggest problem. My work schedule is very hectic, to say the least. However, exercise needn't always mean running on a treadmill or pumping iron in the gym for hours on end. Quick short walks in the park (or to and from the railway station or grocery store) can make a difference. The easiest way to increase your heart rate is to forego the elevator or standing on the escalator and climb up the stairs. It works for me whenever I find myself traveling and lacking time for the gym.

As a parent I recognize that it is also important for my children to be active, whether it's playing soccer, swimming, or ballet for the girls. Building good habits from an early age means that they are more likely to participate in physical activity later in life.

Healthy desserts

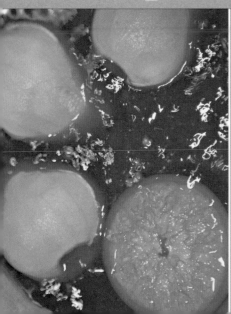

Vanilla panna cotta
with blueberry sauce

blueberries are a great source of antioxidants

Serves 6

2½ cups (600ml) whole or low-fat milk

1 vanilla bean, split

⅔ cup (125g) superfine sugar

4 sheets of leaf gelatin

generous ¾ cup (200ml) plain yogurt

Blueberry sauce:

9oz (250g) blueberries, rinsed and dried

3 tbsp (45ml) superfine sugar or honey

2–3 tbsp (30–45ml) lemon juice

Pour the milk into a pan and scrape in the seeds from the vanilla bean, adding the bean too. Add the sugar and heat gently, stirring until the sugar has dissolved, then bring to a simmer. Meanwhile, soak the gelatin leaves in cold water for a few minutes to soften them.

As soon as the milk begins to bubble, remove the pan from the heat. Drain the gelatin leaves and squeeze out excess water, then add to the hot milk. Stir to dissolve, then let cool before straining through a fine strainer into a bowl.

Add the yogurt to the infused milk (which must have cooled completely). Pour the mixture into 6 pannacotta or dariole molds and set them on a tray. Cover with a large piece of plastic wrap and chill for a few hours until set, or overnight.

For the sauce, put the blueberries, sugar, and lemon juice into a pan. Bring to a simmer and cook for 3 minutes until the berries are soft, but not completely broken down. Transfer to a bowl and let cool, then chill.

To unmold each panna cotta, dip the mold in a bowl of warm water for a few seconds, then invert onto a plate and give it a gentle shake to release. If necessary, dilute the blueberry sauce with a tiny splash of water. Spoon a little sauce around each panna cotta and serve.

Pink grapefruit granita with raspberries

fat free and plenty of vitamin C

Put the grapefruit juice, sugar, and star anise into a pan. Stir over low heat until the sugar has dissolved, then increase the heat slightly and bring a simmer. Remove from the heat as soon as the juice begins to bubble. Let cool completely, then strain and discard the star anise.

Pour the juice into a suitable container and freeze for about 2 hours until it is frozen around the sides and base. Take out of the freezer and use a fork to lightly beat the frozen crystals into the still-liquid center, then return to the freezer. Repeat beating two or three more times until the granita is frozen with a granular texture.

To serve, scrape the granita with a fork, then spoon into chilled serving glasses. Add a few raspberries to each glass, then pour over a little pink champagne if you like. Serve at once.

Variations:

- For a refreshing minty flavor, add a handful of mint leaves in place of the star anise.
- For a citrus granita, use equal parts of orange, grapefruit, and blood orange juice.
- Spike the granita with 2 tbsp (30ml) Campari once the juice has cooled down. Serve drizzled with Campari instead of champagne.

Serves 4

2 cups (500ml) pink grapefruit juice, preferably freshly squeezed and strained (3–4 juicy fruit)

generous 1/3 cup (75g) superfine sugar

2 star anise

handful of raspberries

chilled pink champagne, to serve (optional)

Baked plums
with crushed amaretti

equally delicious with juicy nectarines or peaches

Serves 4

1lb (500g) ripe, but firm, plums

few small pieces of butter, plus extra to grease

2–3 tbsp (30–45ml) crème de cassis or marsala

1oz (30g) amaretti cookies

strained plain yogurt, to serve

Heat the oven to 400°F (200°C). Cut the plums in half and remove the pits. Arrange the plum halves, cut side up, in a lightly buttered baking dish. Drizzle over the liqueur.

Crush the amaretti cookies lightly in a large bowl with the end of a rolling pin. Sprinkle over the plum halves, then dot a small piece of butter on each fruit. Bake for 10 to 15 minutes, depending on the ripeness of the plums, until they are soft but still retain their shape. Let cool slightly.

Serve warm, with a spoonful of yogurt.

Spiced apple cake

deliciously dense and moist, with lots of healthy fiber

Serves 8

2lb (1kg) cooking apples
(about 5 or 6)

¼ cup (50g) superfine sugar

2 tbsp (30ml) butter, plus extra
to grease

2 ripe Braeburn apples

juice of 1 lemon

1⅓ cups (225g) whole wheat flour

4 tsp (20ml) baking powder

½ tsp (2ml) baking soda

¼ tsp (1ml) fine sea salt

scant 1 cup (175g) brown sugar

1 tsp (5ml) ground cinnamon

1 tsp (5ml) ground ginger

½ tsp (2ml) freshly grated nutmeg

½ tsp (2ml) ground cloves

1 large egg, lightly beaten

¼ cup (50ml) light olive oil

2 tbsp (30ml) apricot jelly, to glaze

1–2 tbsp (15–30ml) water

Peel, core, and slice the cooking apples. Place in a wide pan with the sugar and butter. Cook over high heat for 10 to 15 minutes until the apples have broken down to a pulp and any excess water has cooked off. Transfer to a bowl and cool completely. You should have about 1lb (475g) purée.

Heat the oven to 325°F (170°C). Line and lightly grease a 9-inch (23cm) cake pan with a removable bottom. Peel, core, and finely slice the eating apple, using a mandolin or sharp knife. Place in a bowl and pour over most of the lemon juice and a splash of water; set aside.

In a large bowl, mix together the whole wheat flour, baking powder, baking soda, salt, sugar, and ground spices. Make a well in the center and add the egg, olive oil, and apple purée. Fold into the dry ingredients until just combined.

Transfer the mixture to the prepared cake pan and gently level the top with a spatula. Bake the cake for 30 minutes until it feels just firm to the touch in the center. Working quickly, overlap the sliced apples in concentric circles on top, leaving a margin around the edge. Brush the slices with a little lemon juice and return to the oven for another 30 to 35 minutes until a skewer inserted into the center comes out clean.

Let the cake cool slightly before unmolding onto a rack. Warm the apricot jelly with the water, stirring until smooth. Brush over the top of the cake to glaze. Serve warm.

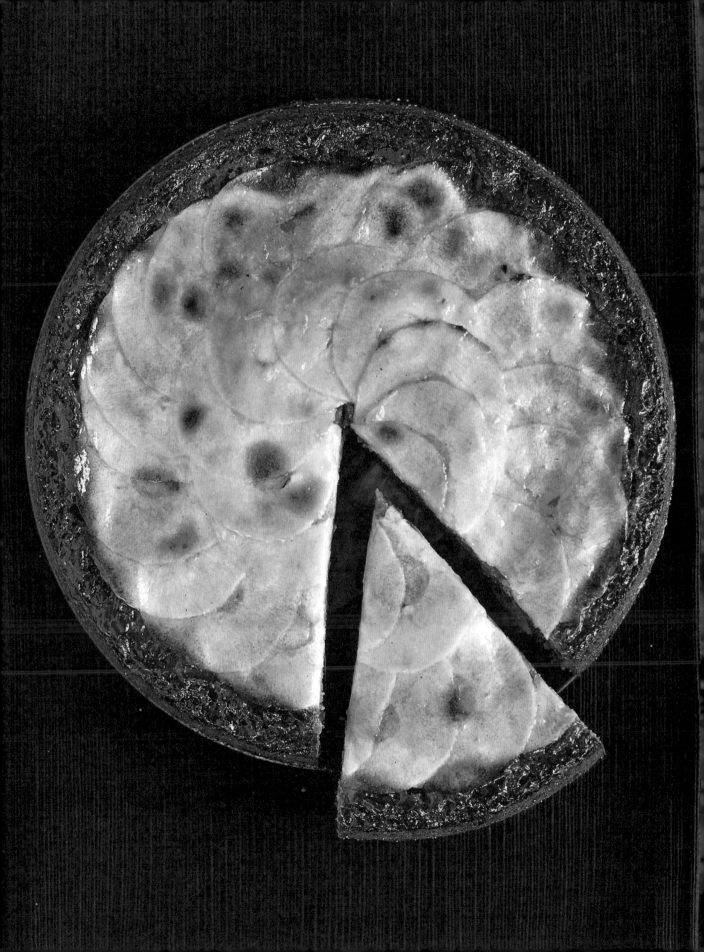

Roasted peaches
with vanilla, spice, and honey

use apple juice for an alcohol-free option

Serves 4

4–5 ripe, but firm, peaches

2 cinnamon sticks

2 star anise

1 vanilla bean, split

3–4 tbsp (45–60ml) runny honey

generous splash of peach liqueur (or peach schnapps or brandy)

plain yogurt, to serve

Heat the oven to 375°F (190°C). Cut the peaches in half and prise out the pits. Slice the peach halves into wedges and arrange on a nonstick baking sheet. Add the spices and vanilla bean, then drizzle over the honey and peach liqueur.

Bake the peaches for 10 to 20 minutes until they are just tender and slightly caramelized around the edges. Remove from the oven and let cool slightly. Serve with a generous spoonful of yogurt, or spooned over very cold yogurt sorbet (see page 243).

Pavlova with creamy roasted rhubarb

Serves 6

4 tsp (20ml) cornstarch, plus 1 tsp (5ml) extra to dust

¾ cup (150g) superfine sugar

3 large egg whites (ideally from eggs about 1 week old)

1 tsp (5ml) vanilla extract

½ tsp (2ml) white wine vinegar

confectioners' sugar, to dust

mint sprigs, to finish

Creamy roasted rhubarb:

1lb (500g) rhubarb, trimmed and roughly chopped

a little butter, to grease

3–4 tbsp (45–60ml) superfine sugar

a little honey, to drizzle

1¾ cups (400ml) strained plain yogurt

Heat the oven to 250°F (140°C). Draw 6 circles, 3 inches (8cm) in diameter, on a sheet of silicone paper or baking parchment. Invert the paper onto a lightly oiled baking sheet and lightly dust with cornstarch. Mix the cornstarch with 1 tbsp (15ml) of the sugar in a small bowl and set aside.

Beat the egg whites in a clean, grease-free bowl to firm peaks, taking care not to overwhisk. Gradually beat in the remaining sugar, 1 tbsp (15ml) at a time, and whisk until thick and glossy. Fold through the cornstarch mixture, vanilla, and vinegar.

Spoon the meringue into a large pastry bag fitted with a ½–⅝-inch (1–1.5cm) plain tip. Pipe concentric circles over each circle to create a disc, then pipe two rings on the rim to form a shell. Bake for 40 to 45 minutes until dry and crisp. Turn off the oven and let the meringues cool slowly inside. (Ideally make them the evening before and let cool in the oven overnight.) Peel the meringues off the paper and store in a container.

For the rhubarb, heat the oven to 400°F (200°C). Place the rhubarb in a lightly buttered roasting pan, sprinkle with the sugar, and toss well. Roast for 15 to 20 minutes until tender. Tip the rhubarb and juices into a bowl, drizzle with honey, and let cool completely.

To serve, ripple the roasted rhubarb and juices through the yogurt. Dust the meringue shells with a little confectioners' sugar and place one on each serving plate. Spoon in the rhubarb and top with a mint sprig.

5 ways with
summer berries

Flavorful, ripe berries are an integral part of my diet in the summer. I swear, there are few better ways to start the day than with an energizing smoothie. I simply throw a variety of berries into the blender and whiz them with some low-fat yogurt and pomegranate or other fruit juice. Packed with vitamins, minerals, antioxidants, and fiber, a berry smoothie is a great health boost.

Blueberries are particularly healthy as they have the highest antioxidant capacity. As such, they help to protect the body from cancer and age-related diseases, and promote a healthy skin, eyes, and brain. Great to snack on, blueberries can also be added to all kinds of desserts, from fruit salads to crumbles and cheesecakes.

1

Berry crumble
Heat oven to 375°F (190°C). For the crumble, put ½ cup (60ml) all-purpose flour and 1 tbsp (25ml) chilled diced unsalted butter in a bowl and rub together with your fingertips to a crumbly texture. Stir in 2 tbsp (30ml) raw brown sugar and 2 tbsp (30ml) rolled oats. Spread out on a baking sheet and bake for 15 minutes or until golden brown and crisp, giving it a stir halfway through.

Divide 1⅓lb (600g) mixed blueberries, blackberries and raspberries between individual ovenproof dishes. Grate a little orange rind over each dish, then halve the orange and squeeze a little juice over. Sprinkle 8 shredded mint leaves over the berries along with 1–2 tbsp (15–30ml) sugar to taste. Top with a layer of crumble. Bake for 10 to 12 minutes, just to warm through. Serve warm with yogurt. **Serves 4**

2

Mixed berry coulis
Put 5oz (150g) mixed strawberries, raspberries, and blueberries into a food processor or blender with 1 tbsp (15ml) confectioners' sugar, 2 tbsp (30ml) lemon juice, and 2 tbsp (30ml) water. Whiz to a purée. If the coulis seems a little too thick, add another 1–2 tbsp (15–30ml) water. Pass the mixture through a strainer. Use to drizzle over ices or cakes. **Serves 2–3**

3 Summer berry and vodka jelly

Dissolve 1 cup (200g) superfine sugar in 2 cups (500ml) water in a pan over low heat. Meanwhile, soak 3 sheets of leaf gelatin in cold water to soften. Bring the sugar syrup to a boil and let boil for a few minutes. Take off the heat, squeeze the gelatin leaves to remove excess water, then add to the sugar syrup, stirring to dissolve. Cool, then mix in 4 tbsp (60ml) vodka.

Mix 7oz (200g) raspberries, (7oz) 200g blueberries, and 14oz (400g) hulled and quartered strawberries in a bowl. Shred a handful of basil leaves and toss with the berries, then divide between 5–6 small serving glasses. Pour over just enough of the cooled vodka syrup to cover the berries. Chill for a few hours until set. **Serves 5–6**

4 Raspberry, mango, and watercress salad

Peel and thinly slice 1 large ripe mango, avoiding the seed. Trim 7oz (200g) watercress, removing the stems. Divide the mango and watercress between individual plates and sprinkle over 3oz (80g) raspberries. For the dressing, whisk 4 tsp (20ml) raspberry vinegar with 4 tbsp (60ml) extra-virgin olive oil, some salt and pepper, and a pinch of superfine sugar to taste. Drizzle over the salad and serve, as an appetizer. **Serves 4**

5 Port and blackberry sauce

Heat 1 tbsp (15ml) olive oil in a pan and sweat 1 minced large shallot with some seasoning for 4 to 6 minutes until soft. Pour in ⅓ cup (75ml) port and let bubble until reduced by two-thirds. Add 5oz (150g) blackberries, ⅔ cup (150ml) chicken stock (see page 249), and 2 tbsp (30ml) red currant jelly. Bring to a simmer and cook for 8 to 10 minutes until thickened to the desired consistency. Strain and serve as an accompaniment to duck, game, and pork. **Serves 4**

Poached pears
in mulled wine

easy prepare-ahead dessert

Serves 4

3 cups (750ml bottle) of red wine

4 tbsp (60ml) superfine sugar

2 cinnamon sticks

½ tsp (2ml) cloves

2 orange slices

1 preserved ginger in syrup, halved

4 ripe, but firm, pears

Pour the red wine into a medium pan and add the sugar, spices, orange slices, and preserved ginger. Slowly bring to a simmer, stirring initially to dissolve the sugar. Simmer gently for 15 to 20 minutes to let the aromatics infuse their flavors into the wine.

Peel each pear, leaving the stalk on, and scoop out the core from the base with a melon baller. Gently lower the pears into the mulled wine. Rest a crumpled piece of waxed paper with a small hole cut out in the center on top; this will help to keep the pears submerged in the liquid.

Poach the pears for 10 to 20 minutes, depending on ripeness. To test, pierce with a fine metal skewer—it should meet with little resistance. Transfer the pears and mulled wine to a large bowl and let cool. Cover with plastc wrap and refrigerate overnight to let the flavors develop.

Serve the pears warm, reheating them gently, or at room temperature, with a scoop of vanilla ice cream or yogurt sorbet (see page 243) if you like.

Camomile and ginger jelly
with ginger melon

fat free and truly refreshing

Serves 4–6

½oz (10g) camomile tea or 2 camomile teabags

scant ½ cup (85g) superfine sugar

finger length piece of gingerroot, thickly sliced

2 cups (500ml) boiling water

3 sheets of leaf gelatin

Ginger melon:

generous ½ cup (75g) superfine sugar

⅓ cup (75ml) water

small piece of gingerroot, peeled and cut into thin sticks

1 charentais or a small honeydew melon

Put the camomile tea, sugar, and ginger into a warmed large teapot. Pour in the boiling water, put the lid on, and let infuse for 4 to 5 minutes. Meanwhile, soak the gelatin leaves in cold water to cover for a few minutes to soften.

Strain the infused tea into a pitcher and discard the tea and ginger pieces. Drain and squeeze out the excess water from the gelatin leaves, then add to the hot tea and stir to dissolve. Let cool completely. Pour into individual serving glasses and chill for 6 hours or longer until the jellies have set.

For the ginger melon, dissolve the sugar in the water in a small pan over low heat, stirring occasionally. Increase the heat and bring to a boil, then add the ginger and simmer for 5 minutes. Remove from the heat and set aside to infuse until cold.

Cut the melon in half and remove the seeds. Scoop out the flesh into balls, using a melon baller, and place in a large bowl. Strain the infused syrup over the melon. Let macerate for 10 minutes.

To serve, spoon a few melon balls onto each jelly and drizzle with a little of the syrup.

Lime mousse

Serves 8

2 sheets of leaf gelatin

juice of 4 limes (about ⅔ cup/150ml)

scant 1 cup (175g) superfine sugar

2 medium egg whites

¾ cup (200ml) reduced-fat crème fraîche

1–2 limes

Soak the gelatin leaves in cold water to cover for a few minutes to soften. Meanwhile, put the lime juice in a measuring cup and top off with cold water to reach a generous ¾ cup (200ml). Pour into a pan and add half the sugar. Stir over low heat to dissolve, then increase the heat and bring to a simmer. Take the pan off the heat.

Drain the gelatin leaves and squeeze out excess water, then add to the lime syrup and stir to dissolve. Let cool completely.

Beat the egg whites in a clean, grease-free bowl with an electric whisk until they form stiff peaks. Beat in the remaining sugar, 1 tbsp (15ml) at a time, until fully incorporated and the meringue is firm.

In another bowl, lightly beat the crème fraîche, then stir in the cooled lime mixture. (The mixture will be quite loose and thin at this stage.) Fold through the meringue, then spoon the mixture into small serving glasses.

Chill the mousses for a few hours to firm up a little. Grate over a little lime rind to finish before serving.

tangy, soft set mousse, rich in vitamin C

Ricotta cheesecake
with orange and cinnamon

low-fat baked cheesecake

Serves 8

Crust:

3 tbsp (45ml) lightly salted butter, melted, plus extra to grease

5oz (150g) reduced-fat graham crackers

1 medium egg white, lightly beaten

Ricotta filling:

1lb (500g) ricotta cheese

8oz (250g) quark

½ cup (100g) superfine sugar

1 tbsp (15ml) cornstarch

3 large eggs

finely grated rind of 1 orange

2–3 tbsp (30–45ml) Grand Marnier or Cointreau, to taste

½ tsp (2ml) ground cinnamon

Oranges in syrup (optional):

4 large oranges

¼ cup (50g) superfine sugar

4 tbsp (60ml) Grand Marnier or Cointreau

Heat the oven to 300°F (150°C). Lightly butter a deep 8-inch (20cm) cake pan with a removable bottom.

For the crust, break up the crackers and whiz in a food processor to fine crumbs. Add the melted butter and pulse until the mixture comes together. Tip into the prepared pan and press down firmly with the back of a spoon to create a neat crust. Stand the pan on a baking sheet and bake for 10 to 12 minutes until lightly browned. As you remove it from the oven, brush the crust with the egg white. Let cool slightly. Clean the processor.

For the ricotta filling, whiz all the ingredients in the food processor until well blended. You may need to stop the machine to scrape down the sides once or twice. Pour the filling over the crust and bake for 30 minutes until it has just set around the sides but is still quite runny in the middle.

Turn off the heat but leave the cheesecake in the oven to cool slowly; the filling will continue to set as it cools. Leave until completely cooled, preferably overnight.

To prepare the oranges if serving, cut away the peel and pith, then slice into circles and place in a bowl. Heat a heavy skillet until hot, add the sugar, and let it caramelize over high heat. Protecting your hand (as the mixture will splutter), add the liqueur and a small splash of water. The caramel may harden, but it will soften and return to a syrup as you stir over low heat. Pour over the orange slices and toss to coat.

To serve, run a knife around the cheesecake and unmold onto a plate. Serve with the oranges in syrup if you wish.

Yogurt sorbet

a refreshing low-fat alternative to ice cream

Pour the water into a heavy pan, add the sugar and liquid glucose, and place over low heat. Stir occasionally until the sugar has dissolved, then increase the heat and boil for 3 to 4 minutes. Remove from the heat and cool completely.

Beat the yogurt and fromage frais together in a bowl until smooth and creamy. Mix in the cooled syrup.

Pour the mixture into an ice-cream machine and churn until almost firm, then scoop the sorbet into a suitable container and freeze for several hours until firm. If you do not have an ice-cream machine, freeze the mixture in a shallow container and beat with a fork several times during freezing.

Delicious served with both hot and cold desserts, or scooped into glasses with fresh fruit.

Variations:

- Purée ½ ripe but firm mango and chop the other half. Fold the purée into the sorbet mixture before freezing; fold in the chopped mango halfway through churning.
- Purée the flesh of 2–3 ripe peeled nectarines or peaches until smooth and fold into the sorbet base before freezing.
- Reduce the water to 1¼ cups (300ml). Add the finely grated rind and juice of 2 limes to the sorbet mixture before freezing. Serve with griddled pineapple wedges.

Serves 6–8

1½ cups (350ml) water

1 cup (225g) superfine sugar

3 tbsp (45ml) liquid glucose

1¼ cups (300ml) plain yogurt

generous ⅓ cup (100ml) fromage frais

Chocolate mousse

Serves 4

5oz (150g) semisweet chocolate, in pieces, plus an extra 1oz (25g) for grating

2 chocolate-coated honeycomb bars

½ cup (100g) superfine sugar

1 tsp (5ml) liquid glucose

2 tbsp (30ml) water

2 large egg whites

generous ⅓ cup (100ml) crème fraîche

1–2 tbsp (15–30ml) Kahlua or other coffee liqueur (optional)

Melt the chocolate in a heatproof bowl set over a pan of simmering water. Meanwhile, put the honeycomb bars into the freezer for 10 minutes. When the chocolate has melted, remove from the heat and set aside.

For the meringue, put the sugar, liquid glucose, and water into a pan and place over low heat until the sugar has dissolved, stirring a couple of times. Increase the heat and boil the syrup until it registers 248°F (120°C) on a sugar thermometer; ie the "hard ball stage," when a little of the hot syrup dropped into a glass of water hardens to a form a clear ball.

Meanwhile, beat the egg whites in a clean, grease-free bowl to stiff peaks. With the beaters working, slowly trickle the hot syrup onto the egg whites. Continue to whisk until the egg whites are smooth, glossy, and have tripled in volume. The sides of the bowl should no longer feel hot.

Add the crème fraîche to the melted chocolate and whisk to combine. Fold the chocolate mixture into the meringue, followed by the coffee liqueur if using.

Remove the wrapper from one of the chilled honeycomb bars and wrap in a clean dish towel. Place on a board and bash lightly with a rolling pin to crush the honeycomb. Open up the dish towel and tip the crushed honeycomb into the mousse, then gently fold through with a spatula.

Spoon the mousse into small serving dishes set on a tray. Grate over a layer of chocolate-coated honeycomb, followed by a layer of chocolate. Chill for a few hours before serving.

Healthy basics

Vegetable stock

Makes about 6 cups (1.5 liters)

3 onions, peeled and roughly chopped

1 leek, washed and roughly chopped

2 celery stalks, roughly chopped

6 carrots, peeled and roughly chopped

1 head of garlic, halved crosswise

1 tsp (5ml) white peppercorns

1 bay leaf

few thyme, basil, tarragon, cilantro, and parsley sprigs, tied together

¾ cup (200ml) dry white wine

sea salt and black pepper

Put the vegetables, garlic, peppercorns,
and bay leaf in a large stockpot and pour on cold water to cover, about 8 cups (2 litres). Bring to the boil, lower the heat to a simmer, and leave to cook gently for 20 minutes. Remove the pan from the heat and add the bundle of herbs, white wine, and a little seasoning. Give the stock a stir and let cool completely.

Chill the stock overnight before straining if
you have time. Pass through a fine strainer into a bowl. Refrigerate and use within 5 days, or freeze in smaller amounts for up to 3 months.

Fish stock

Makes about 4 cups (1 liter)

2 tbsp (30ml) olive oil

1 small onion, peeled and chopped

½ celery stalk, sliced

1 small fennel bulb, chopped

sea salt and black pepper

2lb (1kg) white fish bones and trimmings (or crab or lobster shells)

⅓ cup (75ml) dry white wine

Heat the olive oil in a stockpot and add the
onion, celery, fennel, and a little seasoning. Stir over medium heat for 3 to 4 minutes until the vegetables begin to soften but not brown. Add the fish bones and trimmings and the wine, then pour in enough cold water to cover the ingredients. Simmer for 20 minutes, then remove the pan from the heat and let cool.

Ladle the stock through a fine strainer into a
bowl and discard the solids. Refrigerate and use within 2 days, or freeze in smaller quantities for up to 3 months.

Chicken stock

Makes about 6 cups (1.5 liters)

2 tbsp (30ml) olive oil

1 carrot, peeled and chopped

1 onion, peeled and chopped

2 celery stalks, chopped

1 leek, washed and sliced

1 bay leaf

1 thyme sprig

3 garlic cloves, peeled

2 tbsp (30ml) tomato paste

2 tbsp (30ml) all-purpose flour

2lb (1kg) raw chicken bones

sea salt and black pepper

Heat the olive oil in a large stockpot and add

the vegetables, herbs, and garlic. Cook over medium heat, stirring occasionally, until the vegetables are golden. Stir in the tomato paste and flour and cook for another minute. Add the chicken bones, then pour in enough cold water to cover. Season lightly. Bring to a boil and skim off any scum that rises to the surface. Reduce the heat and leave to simmer gently for 1 hour.

Let the stock stand for a few minutes, then

pass through a fine strainer and let cool. Refrigerate and use within 5 days, or freeze the stock in convenient portions for up to 3 months.

Beef stock

Makes about 6 cups (1.5 liters)

3lb (1.5kg) beef or veal marrow bones, chopped into 2–2½inch pieces

2 tbsp (30ml) olive oil, plus extra to drizzle

2 onions, peeled

2 carrots, peeled

2 celery stalks, peeled

1 large fennel bulb, trimmed

1 tbsp (15ml) tomato paste

3½oz (100g) white mushrooms

1 bay leaf

1 thyme sprig

1 tsp (5ml) black peppercorns

Heat the oven to 425°F (220°C). Put the bones in

a roasting pan and drizzle with a little olive oil. Roast for about 1 hour, turning over halfway, until browned. Meanwhile, cut the onions, carrots, celery and fennel into 2-inch chunks.

Heat the olive oil in a large stockpot and add

the vegetables. Cook, stirring frequently, over high heat until golden brown. Stir in the tomato paste and cook, stirring, for 2 minutes. Add the browned bones and pour in enough water (about 8–10½ cups/2–2.5 liters) to cover them and the vegetables. Bring to a simmer and skim off the froth and scum that rise to the surface. Add the mushrooms, bay leaf, thyme and peppercorns. Simmer for 6 to 8 hours until the stock has a deep, rich flavor.

Leave to stand for a few minutes, then pass the

stock through a fine strainer. Let cool, then refrigerate and use within 5 days, or freeze in smaller portions for up to 3 months.

INDEX

ACKNOWLEDGMENTS

A book of this quality can only be put together with the strength and dedication of the talented team that I am so lucky to be working with. Once again, I am indebted to my "adopted son," Mark Sargeant, who has worked tirelessly on every photo shoot and always manages to lighten the day with his humor. Mark now leaves the family to get married, but remains my right-hand man. I am very grateful to Pat Llewellyn and everyone at Optomen TV for helping me. Pat and I work together almost like tomato and basil in the kitchen. And I owe a special thanks to my dear Emily, for her hard work, patience, and understanding of what precious time I have. Dynamic meetings with her left me enough time to play football ... brilliant, Emily.

A big thank you to Helen Lewis, as always. Helen helped me with my first ever book, so she has been there from the start and knows me inside out, which is apparent throughout this book. I now regard her as an integral member of our kitchen brigade. And to the newly found yummy mummy of the photography world, Jill, who is terrific. Her enthusiasm is infectious, though I cringe when she calls me poppet! And Janet Illsley, for being forever demanding and scrutinizing editorial-wise, a job well done yet again...I think I owe you twelve dinners now, twelve tables for two. And, of course, Anne Furniss and Alison Cathie, for trusting the vision to get behind this campaign.

And thanks to everyone at Gordon Ramsay Holdings, from Gillian Thomson to Chris Hutcheson. Also to Jo Barnes for her strategy and determination to make this book a big hit. And to Tony Turnbull from The Times who has shared my passion. Without all these people listed, this book wouldn't f...... be here!

And finally to my four new sous chefs Jack, Holly, Megan, and Matilda. A huge thanks for tasting all the recipes that your father is cooking ... and under no circumstances do you send any of his food back. Thanks, also, to my mother, Helen, for being a great prop... you may not like having your picture taken Mom, but you look terrific! And last but not least, to the most patient woman in Britain today, my beloved wife Tana.

notes

Recipes give both standard American measures and metric measures. The two sets of measurements are not exact equivalents, so use one or the other, not a combination.

All spoon measures are level unless otherwise stated: 1 tsp = 5ml spoon; 1 tbsp = 15ml spoon.

All herbs are fresh, and all pepper is freshly ground black pepper unless otherwise suggested.

I recommend using free-range eggs. If you are pregnant or in a vulnerable health group, avoid those recipes that contain raw egg whites or lightly cooked eggs.

If possible, buy unwaxed citrus fruit if you are using the rind.

My timings are provided as guidelines, with a description of color or texture where appropriate. Oven timings apply to convection ovens. If using a conventional oven, increase the temperature by 25°F (15°C). Use an oven thermometer to check the accuracy of your oven.

optomen

Optomen Television Limited
1, Valentine Place
London SE1 8QH
www.optomen.com